low fat goes
luscious

lauren oostingh

photography by craig fraser
food styling by abigail donnelly

Dedicated to God, who turns all things to good.

I would like to thank everyone who played a part in putting this
book together and who gave me this wonderful opportunity:
My dear family; my mother; the Struik team, especially Linda,
Joy and Petal; Craig and Abigail; and Lynn Bedford Hall.

I am grateful to Prof. Roy Swank, Prof. E. Fields and Judy
Graham for their lifetime's research into MS and for their help.

For more information about the MS diet, you can contact
Lauren Oostingh via e-mail: laurengo@iafrica.com

First published in the UK in 2003 by
New Holland Publishers (UK) Ltd
Garfield House
86–88 Edgware Road
London W2 2EA
United Kingdom
www.newhollandpublishers.com

First published in 2002
10 9 8 7 6 5 4 3 2 1

Copyright © in published edition: Struik Publishers 2002
Copyright © in text: Lauren Oostingh 2002
Copyright © in photographs: Craig Fraser/Struik Image Library 2002

www.newhollandpublishers.com

Publishing manager: Linda de Villiers
Editor: Joy Clack
Designer: Petal Palmer
Assistant designer: Beverley Dodd
Design assistant: Sean Robertson
Photographer: Craig Fraser
Food stylist: Abigail Donnelly
Proofreader: Brenda Brickman
Indexer: Mary Lennox

Reproduction by Hirt & Carter Cape (Pty) Ltd
Printed and bound by Sing Cheong Printing Co. Ltd

ISBN 1 84330 513 5

Thank you to the following for supplying props:
LIM, Peter Visser, Bright House, The Yellow Door and
Nocturnal Affair.

The following are based on recipes by Judith Wills for
Good Housekeeping magazine, National Magazine Company, UK:
Bean and basil dip (page 39)
Haddock with couscous and crisp greens (page 47)
Saffron and chickpea pilaf (page 69).

CONTENTS

INTRODUCTION

Twelve years ago I was a lavish cook with a large bottom! My dishes were liberally laced with cream, wine, butter and chocolate. After the birth of my first child, it became obvious that all was not well with my health. I was 30 but, as I battled to walk and function, I felt more like 80. A year later, after extensive tests, I was diagnosed with Multiple Sclerosis (MS) and told that nothing could be done for me. Fortunately, God had other plans for me. I found a brilliantly researched book on the success of treating MS with a low-fat, wholefood diet. I just knew this was the way to go as I had seen how changing to a healthy diet had completely reversed my father's crippling gout. I ate my last chocolate, went cold turkey and gave up all my favourite foods. Within three days my MS symptoms began to recede and the improvement was rapid and steady until my health was better than ever before. My bottom became a mere shadow of its former self. But I would still wander around food halls and delicatessens drooling. My passion for cooking couldn't stay dormant for long and I discovered, to my delight, that there were still plenty of foods left to eat and exciting new one's that I'd never even heard of before. Change in tastes came slowly, but it did come. I can honestly say that I far prefer my way of eating now and, given the choice, I would never want to return to my old, unhealthy ways.

This is a collection of low-fat, wholefood recipes that I have put together over the last 11 years. Some of these recipes evolved from experiments that turned out well. The rest are adaptations of recipes that I have found in other cookbooks or old favourites from the past that have been altered to suit my needs. It is surprisingly easy to adapt recipes to suit individual health needs,

left: light lemon mousse tart (page 81)

but when you are new to it, there are flops aplenty. My aim is to try to shorten the learning curve for you and show that healthier food doesn't have to be uninteresting and tasteless. Most of these recipes have been tested on my cooking classes and pronounced fit for human consumption. This book is also for the benefit of others with Multiple Sclerosis, who are usually so horrified by the diet rules they are supposed to follow that they tend to give up before giving it a chance to work for them. It is so much easier to replace the problem foods in your diet with equally delicious, good foods than it is to live with MS, which robs you of so much that makes your life worth living.

The subject of diet is incredibly vast and complex, and many diets conflict so badly that it can become terribly confusing for someone searching for the right path to health. The more I learn about food, the more I realize how much there is to learn and how far I still have to go. One thing I'm sure of, however, is that the healthiest option is to alter your food as little as possible from its natural state. As it comes off a tree or out of the ground, your food is brimful of all the nutrients and enzymes that your body needs to function properly. Anything you do to it will usually only detract from that. For perfectly healthy eating, you don't really need a cookbook. However, being human, we enjoy a bit of spice in our lives. The recipes in this book fall somewhere between the typical western diet and 'the perfect way', and should help to ease the transition from one to the other. Even the treats have nutritional value! Remember though, that for great health these recipes are meant to be that little bit of 'spice' added to a very healthy diet (see My Ideal Diet, page 6). They are not intended to take pride of place on your plate – that is reserved for raw veggies!

MY IDEAL DIET

Despite the confusing contradictions that are often encountered when searching for the perfect eating plan, there is a common thread that runs through all good books on health.

Below is a summary of what I have gleaned from these books over the years. These steps are what I have found really work for me. They keep me full of energy, resistant to illness and at a comfortable weight without any difficulty. These guidelines may sound rather emphatic but don't take them as the last word on healthy eating for I am no expert – rather try them for yourself and see what suits you.

Aim for your diet to comprise at least 50% raw, 'living' food

This may sound impossible at first, but every step that you take in this direction can only be of benefit to you. 'Live' foods are fresh, raw foods that are naturally brimming over with all the ingredients necessary for your body to function properly and to build new cells.

Your body is made up of countless cells that are constantly being replaced. The new cells that are created can only be as good (or bad) as the raw materials that are made available for their formation. Your body is genetically programmed to heal itself and, when provided with good building materials, it will grab the opportunity to do so. *A largely raw diet is therefore the key to a healthy life.*

Raw foods, and green plants in particular, are packed with enzymes, minerals, vitamins, proteins and chlorophyll, all of which are vital for good health. In addition, plants contain countless other health-giving substances that can, for example, have a natural antibiotic effect; offer protection from pollutants and cancer-promoting substances; boost immunity to prevent infections and disease; or slow down the ageing process – to mention just a few.

Raw vegetables should make up the largest part of your *raw* diet, followed by raw fruit, raw vegetable juices (fresh carrot juice, for example) and small quantities of raw seeds, nuts and cold-pressed oils. Obviously meat and foods such as rice and potatoes are not eaten raw, and these should make up a smaller part of your diet. Cooked vegetables also have an important place in the diet, but they should, if possible, be lightly steamed and not boiled and overcooked.

Overcooked and processed food is dead food. High temperatures bring about undesirable changes in foods. This not only dramatically reduces the nutritional value of the food, but can even make the food constituents harmful to the body.

During cooking and processing of food:

- A large percentage of the vitamins is destroyed.
- Amino acids, the building blocks of proteins, can become so denatured that they are unable to be processed by the digestive enzymes.
- Organic minerals can be reduced to inorganic, unusable forms.
- Enzymes, which are necessary for all dismantling and construction work in the body, can be destroyed. No vitamin, mineral, protein or hormone can do its work without the involvement of enzymes.
- The molecular structure of fats changes, which can make them non-assimilable, poisonous, even carcinogenic. Margarine and cooking oils are examples of processed fats.

Eat only small amounts of meat, eggs and dairy products

Eat as little red meat as possible. Eat fish and white meat of organic, free-range chickens instead. Many health experts argue that we don't need meat at all, but should obtain our protein from vegetable sources (pulses, for example) and nuts. These days anything coming from animal sources is likely to be full of antibiotics, growth hormones, preservatives and toxins – it seems advisable to limit our consumption of animal protein and to widen our range of other protein sources.

Eat no more than three eggs (organic, free-range) per week, and not more than one per day.

Eat only fat-free dairy products, and then only in very small quantities, as they are very mucous-forming. Like meat, they can also contain substances that are best avoided. Pasteurising milk changes the calcium to an inorganic form that is not assimilated easily by the body. The calcium in yoghurt is far more available for absorption. Nevertheless, it is preferable to eat more green vegetables for a readily available organic source of calcium. Be careful of replacing milk with a highly processed, low-quality alternative as the ingredients may be just as bad for you.

Eat foods containing unsaturated oils rather than saturated and processed fats

Many people make the mistake of thinking that all fats are bad. This is not the case and, in fact, certain fats are absolutely vital for good health. The brain, for example, is largely composed of lipids (fats) and therefore the right fats are essential for its growth and repair. It is important to learn to distinguish between good and bad fats and not to eat poor quality, low-fat products that are full of artificial ingredients, in preference to high quality essential fats (such as dressings made with good quality cold-pressed oils). In today's world of processed fats, unless you go out of your way to eat the right kind of oil-rich foods you will not be getting enough good fat. Trying to eliminate all fats from your diet will leave you feeling unsatisfied after meals and will rob the body and brain of essential nutrients.

There are three kinds of fat – saturated, monounsaturated and polyunsaturated. These terms refer to the chemical structure of the fats. Monounsaturated and polyunsaturated fats are together known as

unsaturated fats. Fat is made from smaller components called fatty acids. Certain fatty acids, known as essential (EFAs) as they are crucial for normal growth and development, cannot be manufactured by the body and therefore have to be taken in from food sources. EFAs form part of every cell membrane in the body and are also precursors to hormone-like substances called prostaglandins, which play a role in fine-tuning the way the body functions at a cellular and molecular level.

There are two families of essential fatty acids (EFAs), the Omega 6 and Omega 3 families. These are polyunsaturated fatty acids. A good balance of the two must be taken in daily – an imbalance or lack can cause serious health problems. We tend to be deficient in Omega 3 fatty acids in particular. The best, balanced source of both is cold-pressed linseed oil. Flaxseed oil is also very rich in Omega 9 fatty acids and lignans, molecules with anti-viral, anti-fungal, anti-bacterial and anti-cancer properties.

Other sources of these essential fatty acids include:
- Omega 6 – cold-pressed seed oils (sunflower, sesame, for example), evening primrose oil, liver.
- Omega 3 – fish oils (such as salmon oil), small amounts in green vegetables and legumes.

These EFAs are especially important for those with MS, heart disease, ADHD, inflammatory diseases (such as rheumatoid arthritis), depression, PMS and artherosclerosis. Essential fats support the hormones, brain, skin and hair. They help your memory, are anti-inflammatory, build immunity, lower high blood pressure and protect your heart. They also burn fat, help control weight and reduce the risk of allergies, asthma and eczema.

It is recommended that at least 1–2 Tbsp (15–30 ml) of high quality, cold-pressed linseed oil be consumed daily in order to satisfy your body's requirement for *both* families of essential fatty acids. A good alternative to this is combined evening primrose and marine oil capsules – I take six per day!

Monounsaturated fats are not classified as essential as we can manufacture monounsaturated fatty acids (MUFAs) in the body, but they perform some very important functions. It is therefore important to include sources of MUFAs in the diet. The best source is extra virgin cold-pressed olive oil. Olive oil very effectively lowers bad LDL cholesterol in the body while raising the good HDL cholesterol. Other good sources are avocado and raw nuts. (See List 1 on page 13.)

Saturated fat is generally the kind of fat that is hard at room temperature and of animal origin (butter, meat fat, cheese, and so on). Saturated fat is best avoided as much as possible. It is very detrimental to anyone with MS, cancer, heart or cholesterol problems and even healthy people. (See Lists 2 and 3 on page 13.)

Cold-pressed sunflower and/or olive oil can be used instead of margarine or butter for frying or dressing of food. Linseed oil can be added to salads but must never be heated.

Refining and processing of vegetable oils can change the nature of the unsaturated oil. This kind of fat is then called 'trans' fat and is very damaging to your health. Processed, or hydrogenated oils (margarine, for example), behave like saturated fats in the body. Frying is another way to damage otherwise healthy oils. The high temperature causes oxidation of the oil so that, instead of being good for you, it can actually cause harm. Frying is therefore best done in as little oil as possible and avoided wherever possible. *Add oil to food after cooking rather than during cooking. Never re-use oil.* Normal salad and cooking oils are processed using very high temperatures. Cold-pressing of seeds in the production of cold-pressed oils prevents damage to the essential fats in the seeds. These oils must be kept closed, away from light and should be refrigerated to prevent oxidation. When consuming a lot of polyunsaturated oils it is important that you take in sufficient anti-oxidants such as vitamins C and E as they are very susceptible to oxidation.

Minimize your intake of sugar and foods that are high in sugar

The body has no need for refined sugar, as all fruits and carbohydrates break down into simple sugars. Almost every health condition is negatively affected by high sugar consumption. Refined sugar is so denatured and concentrated compared to its original plant form that it behaves almost like a drug and is very addictive. Apparently, just 10 tsp (50 ml) (the amount in one glass of cola) can inhibit the immune system of a child by 33% for a day, and 30 tsp (150 ml) will shut down the immune system for an entire day. A large amount of any sugar, even natural sugar, brings about a significant drop in the efficiency of white blood cells defending the body and therefore compromises immunity.

Small amounts of honey can be used as an alternative to sugar. Use raw honey if available. Raw honey has not been heated and therefore none of its nutrients have been destroyed. Furthermore, the natural sugar in raw honey is released into the bloodstream at a slower rate than that of honey that has been heated.

Avoid artificial sweeteners – they are very detrimental to your health! Natural stevia, if available (at health-food shops), is a far better alternative.

Plenty of fruit can be eaten but spread its consumption throughout the day. Drink only small amounts of pure fruit juices and dilute them with water. Pure, filtered water is still the drink of choice.

Eat complex carbohydrates instead of refined carbohydrates

Foods falling into the complex carbohydrate category are starchy vegetables (squash, potatoes, and so on), grains, pulses, cereals and beans of all kinds.

Choose:
- brown rice over white;
- home-made wholemeal bread over shop-bought white or wholemeal bread (refined bread clogs the intestines and creates excess mucous in your sinus passages);
- wholemeal or whole-rye pasta over white pasta;
- yellow polenta or cornmeal over white cornmeal;
- rolled oats over quick-cooking oats.

Add to your diet pulses and unrefined grains that you've never tried before, such as lentils, chickpeas, barley or quinoa (some are available from healthfood shops only). Foods in this category are good sources of minerals and vitamins and many are significant sources of protein too.

Eat a wide variety of foods in all categories

Eating a wider variety of vegetables, fruits, whole grains, legumes, nuts, seeds, and so on, will ensure that you get a wider range of nutrients. Furthermore, exposing your digestive system to the same foods every day makes you more prone to developing allergies or intolerances to those foods.

Wheat and dairy products are prime examples of foods that are eaten too much and too often, and are the cause of health problems for many people. There is a surprising number of very palatable alternatives to what may seem like indispensable foods in your diet.

Balance your intake of acid- and alkaline-forming foods

Every food you eat tends to be either acid-forming or alkaline-forming. It is advisable to eat in moderation those foods that are liable to leave an acidic deposit in the system, and eat more alkaline-forming foods. A ratio of 80% alkaline- to 20% acid-forming foods is desirable. Excessive acidity lies at the root of many illnesses, including arthritis and rheumatism. Stress causes a further increase in acidity.

As a rough guide, most fruits and vegetables are alkaline-forming, while most animal products, grains, fish, sugar and coffee are acid-forming.

Avoid too much salt

Your body needs sodium, but it must be in a usable organic form. Table salt (sodium chloride) is an inorganic sodium compound that is extremely harmful to the body and causes it to retain fluid in an effort to keep it out of the cells. The sodium/potassium balance in your body is very important for good health. An excessive intake of salt can upset this balance and bring about a potassium deficiency and a subsequent deterioration in health.

Rather use natural sea salt or herb salt, in *small* quantities.

Avoid carbonated soft drinks

All kinds of soft drinks, for example cola and diet cola, are very acidic. Apparently, it takes 32 glasses of water to neutralize one glass of cola. The phosphoric acid in these drinks causes leaching of calcium out of your bones and teeth. Children who drink a lot of fizzy cool drinks are more prone to fractures than those who don't.

Cut down on caffeine and alcohol intake

Drink herbal teas and rooibos tea rather than regular tea or coffee. Restrict alcohol consumption.

Don't cook in non-stick, plastic or aluminium cookware and minimize the use of clingfilm

These materials can contaminate your food with harmful substances. Avoid contact with and ingestion of chemical pollutants.

Take good food supplements

Poor soil and time delay between harvesting and eating fresh produce can mean that our foods are not quite as nutritious as they should be. Good quality, organically grown food supplements can make up any nutritional shortfalls in your diet.

By far the most outstanding food supplement I have ever encountered is a dehydrated powder made from the juice of sprouted, organically grown barley plants. Young barley leaves have been found to be one of the most prolific and balanced sources of nutrients on earth. The powder is produced through a unique spray-drying method that takes place at room temperature and therefore maintains the complete array of nutrients present in the barley leaves.

Add to this some fresh carrot juice and beetroot juice capsules and you have an excellent, concentrated, alkaline-forming supply of nutrients.

Avoid processed and preserved foods

The colourings, additives, preservatives, chemicals (e.g. aluminium in baking powder), and so on, that are so freely used in processed foods create a toxic load on the body. This can lead to health problems ranging from asthma to hyperactivity, birth defects and cancer. *Eat wholefoods that are as unadulterated and as close to their natural state as possible. Start reading labels and question what you put into your body.*

If you are unsure of which ingredients or products are more suited to a healthy diet, turn to My Pantry on pages 93–94 for a list of the ingredients and products I use in my recipes. I have also provided information on where these products can be obtained.

Get your mind right

There is an intimate connection between mind and body, and our health is influenced by our thoughs and emotions. It has been shown that prayer can boost the immune system and that getting rid of stress and negative emotions can bring about healing.

TIPS FOR LOW-FAT EATING

- Spread your oil allowance throughout the day rather than eating it all at one sitting. Plan your meals and oil intake for the day. If you eat a higher fat item at a meal, eat fat-free foods with it rather than other high-fat foods.
- Measure oil by the teaspoon as it cuts down on your oil intake. Drizzle oil over your food using a teaspoon – it will go much further. A splash of oil straight from the bottle can turn out to be a surprising amount.
- Try not to fry in more than 2 tsp (10 ml) oil, whether cooking for one person or 10. As long as your onion is gently fried in oil, the dish will have that fried flavour. A few drops of water can be added to prevent sticking.
- One or two teaspoons of oil drizzled over a low-fat meal just before eating, makes it more satisfying – it creates the impression of a higher fat meal. It is more effective than frying in the equivalent amount of oil.
- Grated apple is a wonderful fat-replacer in baking. It adds moistness without sogginess and doesn't have a dominating flavour.
- A normal cake recipe need never contain more than ¼ cup (60 ml) oil. The rest can be made up with grated apple and/or plain fat-free yoghurt.
- Plain fat-free yoghurt and cottage cheese are great replacements for cream and cream cheese.
- Use a basting brush to lightly oil a frying pan.
- When eating in a restaurant, take along a little bottle of your own cold-pressed oil. Ask, for example, to have a piece of fish fried in a clean pan in a small quantity of your oil. Order baked potato and salad or stir-fried vegetables to go with it. Have fruit for dessert.
- You can maintain your weight while eating low-fat muffins and so on, but to lose weight you need to eat more fruit and salads and less treats.

eat unrefined grains, good oils and fresh, 'living' foods

LOW SATURATED FAT DIET FOR MULTIPLE SCLEROSIS

I would like to share the basics of my MS diet with everyone as not only is it an *extremely* healthy way of eating, but it also helps everyone who follows it properly to shed an enormous amount of excess weight. In this diet, you look at saturated fat content and unsaturated (polyunsaturated and monounsaturated) oil content of foods eaten, rather than the total fat content. You want to eliminate foods containing mainly saturated (bad) fats and ensure sufficient intake of good quality, unsaturated (good) oils, which are used for healing the body and brain. Professor Swank of Oregon Health Sciences University, who developed and researched steps 1–3 (opposite) for MS (and stroke) patients, discovered that they stop MS in its tracks if started early enough and adhered to *rigidly*.

eat plenty of fresh fruit throughout the day

1. Eat a minimum of 4 tsp (20 ml) and a maximum of 10 tsp (50 ml) of *unsaturated oil* daily from sources given in List 1 (page 13).

   NOTE FOR THOSE WITH MS: Cold-pressed sun-flower oil and linseed oil should be your major sources of essential fatty acids as these are very low in saturated fat. Don't overdo the nuts, and eat the oily fish, avocado, olive oil and olives on List 1 in strict moderation only as they contain a slightly higher proportion of saturated fat. Use the sunflower oil option in the recipes most often and the olive oil only occasionally.

2. Minimize intake of foods containing mainly *saturated* fats. Eat only from sources given in List 2 (page 13) – do not eat more than 1 tsp (5 ml) saturated fat in one day. See List 3 (page 13) for a summary of foods that are 'forbidden'.

3. Eliminate all processed foods containing fat or oil. Read labels – watch out for hydrogenated vegetable fat, unspecified vegetable oils, shortening, and so on.

4. Eat a wholefood diet – unprocessed, unpreserved, unadulterated.

5. Add oil after, rather than during cooking as this preserves its beneficial effects. Never re-use oil. Use only cold-pressed oils. Fry at a low temperature – it is less damaging to the oil. Try to eat not more than 1–2 tsp (5–10 ml) heated oil per day.

6. Minimize refined sugar consumption. Even better, cut it out altogether!

7. Supplement your daily diet with Omega 3 and Omega 6 essential fatty acids and anti-oxidants (vitamins C and E).

List 1 – Foods containing mainly unsaturated oil (and minimal saturated fat)

The following quantities of food contain 1 tsp (5 ml) *unsaturated* oil. The saturated fat content may be disregarded if eaten in moderation. This list can be used to calculate the quantity of unsaturated oil in your dishes.

Linseed oil	1 tsp (5 ml)
Sunflower seed oil	1 tsp (5 ml)
Sesame oil	1 tsp (5 ml)
Olive oil	1 tsp (5 ml)
Mayonnaise, home-made	1 tsp (5 ml)
Salad dressing, home-made	1 tsp (5 ml)
Peanut butter, non-hydrogenated	2 tsp (10 ml)
Tahini (sesame seed paste)	2 tsp (10 ml)
Sunflower seeds	1 Tbsp (15 ml)
Sesame seeds	1 Tbsp (15 ml)
Pumpkin seeds	1 Tbsp (15 ml)
Almonds	2 Tbsp (30 ml)
Cashews	2 Tbsp (30 ml)
Pecans	1½ Tbsp (22.5 ml)
Walnuts	1½ Tbsp (22.5 ml)
Hazelnuts	1½ Tbsp (22.5 ml)
Peanuts, unroasted	15 g
Salmon	60 g
Trout	60 g
Herring	30 g
Mackerel	30 g
Avocado	45 g
Olives (black)	3 medium
Olives (green)	6 medium

Example 1: If you eat 2 tsp (10 ml) peanut butter you have effectively taken in 1 tsp (5 ml) unsaturated oil.

Example 2: If a muffin recipe contains ¼ cup (60 ml) oil and 30 g pecan nuts and makes 6 muffins, 1 muffin will contain 2 tsp (10 ml) oil and 5 g nuts = 2 tsp (10 ml) + ½ tsp (2.5 ml) = 2½ tsp (12.5 ml) unsaturated oil.

List 2 – Allowed foods containing mainly saturated fats

The following quantities of food contain 1 tsp (5 ml) *saturated* fat.

Eggs	1 egg
Chicken liver	90 g

Example: If you eat 90 g chicken liver you have effectively taken in 1 tsp (5 ml) saturated fat.

Note: *Three eggs may be eaten per week, but not more than 1 egg per day. Liver may be eaten once a week. Do not eat eggs and liver on the same day.*

List 3 – Forbidden foods containing saturated or processed fats

Butter, all margarines and butter substitutes
All low-fat and full cream dairy products
Imitation dairy products containing refined oils, such as coffee creamer, soya, oat and rice milks
All red meat, pork and dark meat and skin of chicken or turkey
All shop-bought biscuits, cakes, breads containing any fat or oil
All refined oils, such as rapeseed and sunflower cooking oil
All snacks or sweets containing fat or oil, such as crisps and chocolates
Coconut and commercially roasted nuts

List 4 – Allowed foods

All fruits except coconut
All vegetables
Fat-free dairy products
Chicken breast, all fish and seafood
All unrefined grains and pulses
Raw nuts from List 1
Eggs (3 per week)
Chicken liver and ostrich fillet (occasionally)

OFF TO A

GOOD START

Eating only fruit until lunchtime does not

suit everyone. It's great to start off with, but

you may find yourself becoming weak and

shaky unless you follow it with something a

little more substantial. Carrot juice, crisp

nuts, crunchy muesli, organic eggs, colourful

smoothies. Indulge yourself!

left: smoothie (page 18)

home-made muesli

A comment I received from one of the students on my very first cooking course was 'I don't eat muesli'. Well, she does now! This makes a very satisfying breakfast that keeps the hunger pangs at bay for hours. These quantities are approximate and can be adjusted to suit individual tastes.

SERVES 1

¾ cup (190 ml) raw rolled oats, preferably soaked overnight
4 Tbsp (20 ml) raw nuts, chopped
(almonds, pecans, hazelnuts, cashews, and so on)
1 Tbsp (15 ml) sunflower seeds
4 chopped dates or a small handful of raisins
1 apple, grated (optional)

ONE of the following:
pure fruit juice, diluted OR
skimmed milk, soya milk, rice milk or oat milk OR
plain fat-free yoghurt diluted with a little water OR
filtered water (if you're new to health food, don't try this yet!)

Put all the dry ingredients in a cereal bowl and mix with diluted fruit juice, milk of choice, yoghurt or water.

FAT AND OIL CONTENT
Unsaturated oil – 2 tsp (10 ml)
Saturated fat – may be disregarded

NOTE: Soya, oat and rice milk are not suitable for those with MS if they contain refined vegetable oils.

granola

This is a slightly healthier version of the high-fat, overly sweet granolas that you can buy in supermarkets. It's great as an occasional treat (emphasis on occasional).

MAKES 8 CUPS

6 cups (6 x 250 ml) raw rolled oats
2 cups (500 ml) wheat flakes without added sugar
¼ cup (60 ml) honey
8 tsp (40 ml) cold-pressed sunflower oil
½ cup (125 ml) raisins
16 tsp (80 ml) chopped nuts (pecans, almonds, etc)
¼ cup (60 ml) sunflower seeds

Put the oats and wheat flakes into a large baking dish or onto a baking sheet (not aluminium). Drizzle honey and oil over the cereal mixture and stir until well mixed. Bake at 140–160 °C (275–325 °F) for about 45 minutes, stirring every 15 minutes, until golden.

When cooked, add the raisins, chopped nuts and sunflower seeds. Allow to cool completely before storing in an airtight container.

Serve with skimmed milk (or soya, rice or oat milk).

FAT AND OIL CONTENT IN 1 CUP (250 ML) GRANOLA
Unsaturated oil – 2 tsp (10 ml)
Saturated fat – may be disregarded

NOTE: The nuts and seeds can be roasted with the oat mixture, but the heating process denatures the oils in the nuts, thereby rendering them less healthy. It's your choice!

home-made muesli

smoothie

This is my favourite breakfast, and is a quick way of eating your cereal, fruit and nuts in five minutes flat – perfect for the rushed executive or harassed housewife! You also sidestep the need for milk altogether.

SERVES 1

1 Tbsp (15 ml) sunflower seeds
4 tsp (20 ml) nuts (pecans, almonds, hazelnuts, and so on)
a handful of raw rolled oats, preferably soaked overnight
½ small papaya and 1 banana, sliced OR
1 small mango, 1 banana and 1 small apple, sliced

NOTE: Banana gives great results. If you choose to use pineapple, use only a small slice to prevent a very acid-tasting smoothie.

Process the sunflower seeds, nuts and oats (if not soaked) in a food processor until very finely chopped. Add the fruit and process until smooth. If the oats have not been soaked, add about ¼ cup (60 ml) water to give the smoothie the desired consistency. Don't make it too watery – it must go down easily without being unpleasantly thick. Serve immediately.

FAT AND OIL CONTENT
Unsaturated oil – 2 tsp (10 ml)
Saturated fat – may be disregarded

nick's pikelets

A friend's son promised to make pikelets for tea. The dictionary describes a pike as a large, voracious fish, so you can imagine my relief when the pikelets turned out to be the most delectable crumpets.

MAKES 20 PIKELETS

½ cup (125 ml) wholemeal flour
1½ cups (375 ml) raw rolled oats
½ tsp (2.5 ml) bicarbonate of soda
½ tsp (2.5 ml) salt
1 egg
1 Tbsp (15 ml) cold-pressed sunflower oil
1 Tbsp (15 ml) honey
2 cups (500 ml) filtered water
cold-pressed sunflower oil for frying

Mix all the ingredients, except the oil for frying, in a large mixing bowl and set aside for 5 minutes.

Brush a heavy-based frying pan with a thin film of oil, and heat. Drop dessertspoonsful of batter into the pan. As soon as the pikelets are sizzling, reduce the heat to low. Add a little more oil only when necessary. Serve hot with honey, cinnamon and a squeeze of lemon. Sugar-free jam is also delicious.

FAT AND OIL CONTENT OF ENTIRE MIXTURE
Unsaturated oil – 3 tsp (15 ml) + 1 tsp (5 ml) per tsp oil used for frying
Saturated fat – 1 tsp (5 ml)

other breakfast ideas

Combine a couple of these ideas if you're ravenous in the morning.

Fruit salad: mango, watermelon, grapes, pineapple, papaya, peaches, berries, banana, kiwi fruit, grated apple and pineapple.

A few pieces of fruit and a handful of sunflower seeds and raw nuts.

Sautéed mushrooms on unbuttered toast – use a maximum of 2 tsp (10 ml) oil to cook.

Scrambled or boiled egg on unbuttered wholemeal toast.

Mashed avocado, seasoned with lemon juice and herb salt or sea salt, served on unbuttered home-made wholemeal toast, or rice cakes.

Home-made bread with a spreading of tahini and sugar-free jam.

Sorghum meal porridge from the healthfood shop, cornmeal or oat porridge with honey and skimmed milk (or soya or nut milk). Home-made cashew-nut milk is creamy and delicious. It can be made by processing ¼ cup (60 ml) raw cashews in a food processor until 'powdered' and then adding a drop of honey and ¼–½ cup (60–125 ml) water.

Plain fat-free yoghurt (with live cultures) blended with honey and fruit (strawberries, frozen banana and so on), or sprinkled with chopped nuts, honey and a little Granola (pg 16).

Freshly made carrot juice with a heaped teaspoon or two of sprouted barley juice powder.

Believe it or not, stir-fried vegetables can make a very tasty, alkaline breakfast, especially for those not enjoying great health. They can be combined with polenta, brown rice and/or tofu (marinated in a little soy sauce).

Polenta with a home-made tomato and onion sauce, or a drizzle of olive oil and a sprinkling of herb salt or sea salt.

Half a grapefruit with a little honey drizzled over it.

fruit salad

LIGHT AND
EASY

Sometimes, especially at weekends, it's great to break with routine and go for something simpler without sacrificing taste and nutritional value. Bowls of thick, nourishing soup with hot toast are so good on a winter's day. Big slices of pizza (page 24) can be eaten without a shred of guilt. The mackerel soufflés (page 27) make an excellent lunch or light supper if served with a salad, and can also be a delicious starter. Falafel (page 26) is good at any time and can take the place of meat.

left: open sandwich topped with pear, cottage cheese, celery, pecan nuts and beansprouts (page 27)

spicy tomato soup

The delicious combination of white wine and spices is what sets this soup apart from a typical tomato soup. It is incredibly quick and easy to make, and can be transformed into a seafood bisque with the addition of some fish or prawns.

SERVES 4

1½ large onions, finely chopped
1 tsp (5 ml) crushed garlic
2 tsp (10 ml) cold-pressed olive or sunflower oil
2 small carrots, grated
3 medium, ripe tomatoes, finely chopped
½ stick celery (leaves included), finely chopped
½ cup (125 ml) tomato purée (without additives)
2 tsp (10 ml) honey
50 x 20 mm strip lemon peel
¼ tsp (1 ml) saffron powder or turmeric
¼ tsp (1 ml) mild curry powder
⅛ tsp hot chilli condiment
⅛ tsp ground cumin
¼ cup (125 ml) white wine
2 cups (500 ml) filtered water
1 tsp (5 ml) herb salt or sea salt to taste
freshly ground black pepper to taste
chopped fresh parsley to garnish

Using a large pan with a lid, gently fry the onions and garlic in the oil for 5 minutes. Add all the remaining ingredients, except the pepper and parsley, and simmer, covered, for 30 minutes until the onion is tender. Discard the lemon peel. The soup can be blended in a food processor or with a hand-held blender for a smoother consistency. Serve piping hot with a sprinkling of black pepper and chopped parsley.

FAT AND OIL CONTENT OF ENTIRE DISH
Unsaturated oil – 2 tsp (10 ml)
Saturated fat – may be disregarded

leek and mushroom soup with creamy avocado

Where a swirl of cream is called for and fat-free milk just doesn't do the trick, try a swirl of puréed avocado. I find it quite magnificent.

SERVES 4

1 tsp (5 ml) crushed garlic
½ tsp (2.5 ml) mild curry powder
300 g leeks, well washed and sliced
1 medium onion, chopped
2 tsp (10 ml) cold-pressed olive or sunflower oil
2 large potatoes, peeled and diced
125–250 g white button mushrooms, sliced
2½ cups (625 ml) filtered water
1–2 tsp (5–10 ml) herb salt or sea salt to taste
½ avocado, puréed with a fork just before serving
freshly ground black pepper to taste
a few sprigs of fresh parsley, chopped (optional)

In a large pan with a lid, gently fry the garlic, curry powder, leeks and onion in the oil for a few minutes. Add the potatoes, mushrooms, water and herb salt or sea salt. Bring to the boil, reduce the heat and simmer, covered, for about 20 minutes until the vegetables are tender. Leave to cool a little before blending with a hand-held blender. Reheat just before serving, remove from the heat and whisk in the puréed avocado (the avocado should not be heated for too long). Finish with a little ground black pepper and a sprinkling of parsley.

FAT AND OIL CONTENT OF ENTIRE DISH
Unsaturated oil – 4 tsp (20 ml)
Saturated fat – may be disregarded

hearty vegetable soup

On cold winter days, a bowl of thick vegetable soup is so satisfying, especially when served with home-made wholemeal toast drizzled with a little garlicky olive oil.

SERVES 6

1 tsp (5 ml) crushed garlic
1 large onion, chopped
2 large leeks, chopped
1–2 sticks celery (leaves included), chopped
2 tsp (10 ml) cold-pressed sunflower oil
½ tsp (2.5 ml) mild curry powder
6–8 courgettes, chopped into 20 mm pieces
½ large or 1 small squash, peeled and cubed
2 potatoes, peeled and sliced
250 g white button mushrooms, sliced
2 medium tomatoes, chopped
½ small cauliflower, broken into florets (optional)
3 small carrots, sliced (optional)
1 x 410 g can asparagus pieces (optional)
2 chicken breasts, sliced crossways into thin strips (optional)
filtered water
herb salt or sea salt and freshly ground black pepper to taste
a dash of MSG-free soy sauce (optional)

In a large pan with a lid, gently fry the garlic, onion, leeks and celery in the oil. After about 5 minutes, add the curry powder, courgettes, squash, potatoes, mushrooms, tomatoes, and optional cauliflower, carrots, asparagus and chicken breasts. Add sufficient filtered water to cover. Bring to the boil, then reduce the heat and simmer until the vegetables are *just* cooked. Add more water if the soup looks too thick.

Add seasoning and check for taste. Add a tablespoon or two of soy sauce if it doesn't taste 'meaty' enough.

Allow to cool a little before blending to a smooth, thick consistency with a hand-held blender. Reheat before serving.

If not using immediately, transfer the soup to a suitable container with a lid and refrigerate. This soup also freezes well.

FAT AND OIL CONTENT OF ENTIRE DISH
Unsaturated oil – 2 tsp (10 ml)
Saturated fat – may be disregarded

NOTE: The herb salt used in these soup recipes is a replacement for stock cubes, so you need to be quite generous with the quantity used.

wholemeal pizza

I tried this out on my pizza-loving family and it was a resounding hit with all except four-year-old Kirsty, who hasn't yet acquired a taste for olives. Twelve-year-old Bryony pronounced it 'better than take-aways'. My husband, who tends to be suspicious of my 'healthy alternatives', asked for seconds and thirds.

SERVES 4

pizza base

3 cups (750 ml) wholemeal flour
2 tsp (10 ml) instant yeast
1 tsp (5 ml) herb salt or sea salt
½ Tbsp (7.5 ml) honey
±1½ cups (375 ml) tepid filtered water

topping (all quantities are approximate)

2 Tbsp (30 ml) tomato purée or 1 x 50 g sachet
a sprinkling of dried oregano
½ cup (125 ml) chopped onion
125 g white button mushrooms, sliced
½ red pepper, seeded and sliced
12 kalamata olives, stoned and quartered
1 x 170 g can tuna in brine, drained
100 g canned asparagus tips
lots of crushed garlic
garlic and herb seasoning (optional)
2 Tbsp (30 ml) cold-pressed olive or sunflower oil, or more if desired

OTHER TOPPING IDEAS: Roasted vegetables, canned artichokes, small slices of tofu marinated in soy sauce.

Preheat the oven to 180 °C (350 °F).

Grease a large, non-aluminium baking tin or baking dish (about 30 x 40 cm) with cold-pressed oil and coat with a layer of flour. Shake to discard excess flour.

To prepare the base, mix the flour, yeast, salt and honey in a large mixing bowl. Add ½ cup (125 ml) tepid water and knead with your hands.

Add the remaining water a little at a time to make a soft but pliable dough. If you make it too wet, add a little more flour. Press the dough gently into the tin. Make the base as thin as possible – about 5 mm thick. Leave it to rise in a warm place for about 10 minutes while you prepare the topping.

When you are ready, apply the topping. Gently spread a thin layer of tomato purée over the pizza base with a knife. Add the remaining topping ingredients in the order given alongside, then drizzle the oil over the pizza.

Return the pizza to a warm place for 10–15 minutes until doubled in size and soft and spongy to the touch. Transfer immediately to the oven and bake for 15 minutes, or bake for 10 minutes and grill for 5 minutes. Don't overcook the base.

Remove the pizza from the oven, drizzle more oil over the top if desired and serve.

FAT AND OIL CONTENT OF ENTIRE PIZZA

Unsaturated oil – 10 tsp (50 ml) + 1 tsp (5 ml) per tsp oil added

Saturated fat – may be disregarded if eaten in moderation

wholemeal pizza

falafel

These are little fritters made from chickpeas (also known as garbanzo beans). They are very nutritious and truly delicious with their interesting Middle Eastern spices. You are unlikely to get your family to eat a single boiled chickpea, but I've found that even children devour them in this form.

MAKES 10–12 (SERVES 4)

1 cup (250 ml) dried chickpeas, soaked overnight in water – should produce 2 cups (500 ml) soaked
½ tsp (2.5 ml) crushed garlic
½ small onion, roughly chopped
1 jumbo egg
½ tsp (2.5 ml) cumin powder
½ tsp (2.5 ml) ground coriander
1 Tbsp (15 ml) chopped fresh parsley (optional)
1 tsp (5 ml) herb salt or sea salt
freshly ground black pepper
¼ cup (60 ml) plain fat-free yoghurt to improve consistency of the mixture
cold-pressed sunflower or olive oil for frying
lemon slices

Boil the soaked chickpeas for about 1 hour, or until tender. Discard the water, rinse off any scum that has collected and drain.
Blend the chickpeas, garlic and onion in a food processor until finely chopped. Add the egg, cumin, coriander, parsley (if using) and seasoning and blend.
Add the yoghurt a spoon at a time to achieve the desired consistency – it mustn't be too dry or too sloppy.
Heat 1 tsp (5 ml) oil in a large frying pan, and (using a dessertspoon) add small, flat cakes of the mixture. The yoghurt can make the falafel break quite easily so handle them gently.

falafel

Once the cakes are sizzling nicely, turn the temperature down to low immediately. When the undersides are golden, add 1 tsp (5 ml) more oil and turn the cakes over to fry the other side.
Squeeze a generous quantity of lemon juice over the falafel before eating. A little more oil may be drizzled over them just before eating if too dry. Alternatively, serve with a little yoghurt.

FAT AND OIL CONTENT OF ENTIRE BATCH
Unsaturated oil – 1 tsp (5 ml) per tsp oil used
Saturated fat – 1 tsp (5 ml)

NOTE: This mixture freezes well and can be frozen as individual patties, separated by baking paper, in an airtight container.

smoked peppered mackerel soufflés

What I was actually trying to do here was make savoury muffins. The first batch needed to be sipped with a straw. The second batch turned out to be the most delicious soufflés.

MAKES 4 INDIVIDUAL SOUFFLÉS

250 g potatoes, steamed and mashed by hand
(makes 1 cup/250 ml)
¼ tsp (1 ml) crushed garlic
½ onion, finely chopped
1 large egg
1 Tbsp (15 ml) cold-pressed sunflower or olive oil
¼ cup (60 ml) wholemeal flour
90 g smoked mackerel, flaked
½ tsp (2.5 ml) bicarbonate of soda
1 Tbsp (15 ml) chopped fresh parsley
½ cup (125 ml) plain fat-free yoghurt
lemon slices

Preheat the oven to 180 °C (350 °F). Lightly oil four ramekins and coat each one with flour by shaking a small handful around the inside. Discard excess.
Combine all the ingredients in a mixing bowl and mix well with a fork.
Spoon the mixture into the ramekins, then bake until the top is golden (about 45 minutes). Don't open the oven during cooking because they'll collapse!
The soufflés can be served in the ramekins or they can be turned out onto plates. Serve with lemon slices.

FAT AND OIL CONTENT OF 1 SOUFFLÉ
Unsaturated oil – 1½ tsp (7.5 ml)
Saturated fat in egg – ¼ tsp (1.25 ml)

open sandwich toppings

Tuna salad: Tuna and home-made mayonnaise topped with salad.

Egg mayonnaise: As above but using hard-boiled egg.

Chicken mayonnaise: Thinly sliced chicken breast, stir-fried in 1 tsp (5 ml) cold-pressed oil and a dash of soy sauce, mixed with a little home-made mayonnaise and topped with shredded salad leaves.

Avocado and smoked mackerel: Avocado mashed with lemon juice and topped with a little smoked, flaked mackerel. This also makes a very nice snack when entertaining.

Pear, cottage cheese, celery and pecan nuts: Toast, thickly spread with plain fat-free cottage cheese or Hummus (page 39). Long, thin pear slices arranged on top and sprinkled with chopped celery, pecans and beansprouts (optional). Topped with a little Traditional Salad Dressing (page 37).

Mushroom burger: Sliced tomato, sliced red onion and/or mashed avocado, topped with fat-free grilled mushrooms and home-made mayonnaise.

NOTE: Those with MS should eat avocado and mackerel in moderation only as they contain some saturated fats.

SOMETHING ON THE SIDE

Raw food can change your life! After reading about the amazing benefits of raw food, I determined to put this new knowledge into practice while looking after an exhausted, pregnant friend. The results of this new way of eating were astounding – within a day or two she had regained all her energy and the colour had returned to her cheeks.

Dressings play an important part in a raw diet as they are a good way of taking in your essential fatty acids and also make even the most uninviting raw vegetable more appetizing. Dips are a great replacement for butter and also add interest to salads and pastas.

left: raw energy salad (page 30)

raw energy salad

The best way to recharge your batteries at lunchtime is to toss out the 'salad roll' – a misnomer if ever I heard one – and replace it with a glass of freshly made carrot juice followed by a *real* salad. You'll be amazed at what it does for your energy levels and how much you enjoy it. Serve your salad with a couple of teaspoons of salad dressing drizzled over it or topped with a dollop of one of the dips. You can never overeat on raw veggies so pile your plate high! *Most importantly*, make it interesting so that you won't raid the fridge out of desperation just before supper.

To a bed of *mixed* lettuce leaves add at least THREE of the following raw vegetables:

julienned or grated carrots
small broccoli florets
small cauliflower florets
raw corn cut off the cob OR baby sweetcorn
baby asparagus spears
cherry tomatoes or sliced tomato
mangetout
julienned or grated courgettes
sliced green beans
finely shredded spinach
grated beetroot
finely shredded beetroot greens (leaves)
radishes
chopped celery
slivers of red, yellow or green pepper
cucumber slices
onion rings
sliced mushrooms
sprouts

If you're anything like me, salad alone will not satisfy you for long, so it is a good idea to serve it with one of the following (make sure that the quantity of salad equals or exceeds the quantity of accompaniments):

home-made bread (no butter)
brown rice
barley
couscous
steamed, sliced potatoes
baked potatoes or baked whole squash
baked squash chips or potato chips
   (see note on page 60)
millet
polenta

Arrange the salad attractively on a plate and garnish with fresh herbs, if available.

If desired, your salad can be arranged on top of the accompanying starch and about 4 tsp (20 ml) Traditional Salad Dressing (page 37) poured over the whole meal. I find that this cuts down on the amount of dressing required. Mayonnaise, although delicious, doesn't spread as easily as salad dressing and it is therefore easy to use too much. I find that mayonnaise is best used in small quantities and mixed in with tuna, egg or chicken strips, for example, and then added to the salad. That way you can really taste it without overdoing it.

For an extra-special salad add one of the following:

Avocado (seasoned with lemon and herb salt or sea salt and spread on bread under salad, if desired).

Tofu marinated in soy sauce and olive oil (lemon juice and garlic too, if desired) – tofu is soya bean curd that looks like feta cheese but has very little taste. It takes on the flavour of whatever is added to it.

Tuna in brine (mixed with a few teaspoons of Home-made Garlic Mayonnaise, page 37, if desired).

Raw nuts or seeds (cashews, pecans, sunflower seeds).

Smoked mackerel or salmon – eat smoked food only occasionally.

Boiled egg (mixed with a few teaspoons of garlic mayonnaise and spread on bread under salad, if desired).

Strips of chicken breast stir-fried in garlic, cold-pressed oil and soy sauce.

Olives.

Home-made Preserved Lemons (page 34), chopped.

Home-made marinated aubergines or mushrooms – sliced raw mushrooms or steamed slices of aubergine marinated in Traditional Salad Dressing (page 37).

Slices of steamed beetroot and a little finely chopped onion marinated in Traditional Salad Dressing (page 37).

NOTE: Many experts agree that it is preferable for digestion and fat loss to eat *either* protein *or* starch with your salad. Try it for yourself and see if it makes a difference for you.

Crudités

Instead of the customary plate of crisps and packet dip, I occasionally serve dinner guests a large platter of brightly coloured, raw vegetable and fruit crudités. I arrange them on a bed of lettuce leaves in strips of differing colours around bowls of dips. Garnished with fresh herbs, it can be a work of art and nature has done all the work! It is always amusing to watch professing non-salad-eaters wolf down a plate of these. I choose my vegetables carefully because I'm sure you, too, will have noticed the forlorn pile of raw cauliflower florets and tough chunks of celery that remain untouched.

crudités

waldorf salad

This salad has great visual appeal, especially when a variety of colourful ingredients is used. On one occasion, a few strawberries found their way into my salad and it looked amazing. Even those who are not particularly keen on salad will be tempted to dip into this work of art!

SERVES 4–6

3–4 apples, peeled and diced
Traditional Salad Dressing or Home-made Garlic Mayonnaise (page 37)
2 sticks celery, sliced (the leaves can be used to garnish)
4 Tbsp (60 ml) pecan nuts, chopped
¼ cup (60 ml) raisins
any other colourful additions that you fancy, such as sliced red pepper, radishes, strawberries, grapes (just use your imagination – there are no rules)
1 packet mixed lettuce leaves or 1 small lettuce
1 x 250 g tub plain fat-free chunky cottage cheese

To prevent discoloration of the apple, immediately put the cut pieces in a medium-sized bowl and pour over 4–6 tsp (20–30 ml) dressing or mayonnaise and toss to ensure a thorough coating.

Add the celery, nuts, raisins and your choice of fruit and vegetables to the apple, and mix.

Arrange the lettuce leaves on a platter and pile the cottage cheese in the centre. Surround the cottage cheese with the apple mixture.

FAT AND OIL CONTENT OF ENTIRE SALAD
Unsaturated oil – 3 tsp (15 ml) + 1 tsp (5 ml) per tsp dressing or mayonnaise added
Saturated fat – may be disregarded

russian cabbage and pineapple salad

I find that cabbage needs something sweet with it to take away the aftertaste it can leave. This sweet, tangy Russian salad does just that. It is important not to use too much cabbage.

SERVES 4

1½ baby cabbages or ½ small cabbage, grated in a food processor
½ small pineapple, peeled and finely diced
¼–½ green pepper, seeded and cut into thin strips
2 Tbsp (30 ml) raisins
2–3 gherkins, sliced
Traditional Salad Dressing (page 37)
a few onion rings to garnish (optional)

Mix all the ingredients, except the salad dressing and onion rings, in a salad bowl.

Pour over just enough dressing to coat the salad without drowning it (6–8 tsp/30–40 ml) and toss lightly. For this particular salad you may prefer to use cider vinegar rather than lemon juice in the dressing.

Garnish with onion rings if desired.

FAT AND OIL CONTENT OF ENTIRE SALAD
Unsaturated oil – 1 tsp (5 ml) per tsp of dressing added
Saturated fat – may be disregarded

waldorf salad

cauliflower and broccoli salad with banana and dates

The sweet taste and soft texture of the bananas and dates perfectly complement the slightly harsher taste and crunchiness of the broccoli and cauliflower. It is preferable to use raw vegetables, but *very lightly* steamed vegetables can also be used.

SERVES 4–6

½ small head cauliflower, broken into small florets
1 head broccoli (about 12 cm diameter),
broken into small florets
2 bananas, sliced
12 dates, chopped
2 Tbsp (30 ml) sunflower seeds, toasted
at 180 °C (350 °F) until golden
Traditional Salad Dressing (page 37)

If lightly steamed vegetables are preferred, place the vegetables in a steamer over boiling water for a maximum of 1 minute. Remove and immediately refresh under cold running water.

In a salad bowl, mix the broccoli and cauliflower with the bananas, dates and seeds. Add the dressing and gently toss the salad to coat the ingredients.

FAT AND OIL CONTENT OF ENTIRE DISH
Unsaturated oil – 2 tsp (10 ml) + 1 tsp (5 ml) per tsp dressing added
Saturated fat – may be disregarded

preserved lemons

These fit into the same category as capers, gherkins, anchovies and olives. Their unique flavour will enhance many dishes, especially salads. I always have a jar of them pickling away in my fridge.

2 large ripe lemons, washed and cut into 8 wedges
¼ cup (60 ml) coarse salt
1 cup (250 ml) freshly squeezed lemon juice
(don't use bottled lemon juice)
½ cup (125 ml) cold-pressed olive oil
750 ml capacity small glass preserving jar
(with a rubber seal)

Place a layer of lemon wedges in the preserving jar and sprinkle with a layer of coarse salt. Repeat the layers until you have used up all the lemons and salt.

Pour over the lemon juice, then top up with olive oil – make sure the lemons are completely covered.

Store at room temperature for 7–10 days, inverting the container each day, then gently remove and discard the flesh, leaving only the peel in the oil-lemon juice mixture. Store in the refrigerator (it should keep for up to six months).

FAT AND OIL CONTENT
May be disregarded

red pepper, tomato and preserved lemon relish

My mother keeps a file of interesting sounding recipes that she has every intention of trying – some of these date back to 1965 and the paper is brittle and yellowed! I saved this delicious relish from obscurity by short-circuiting her 'testing' procedure. A little forethought regarding the preparation of the lemons is required the first time you make it, but apart from that it is simple and scrumptious.

SERVES 4 (A LITTLE GOES A LONG WAY)

1 red pepper
150 g cherry tomatoes, quartered OR
1½ ripe, red tomatoes, cubed
⅛ Preserved Lemon, finely diced (page 34)
½ Tbsp (7.5 ml) chopped onion (preferably red onion)
2 tsp (10 ml) cold-pressed olive or sunflower oil
1 tsp (5 ml) freshly squeezed lemon juice
⅛–¼ tsp ground cumin
¼ tsp (1 ml) herb salt or sea salt to taste
a large pinch of paprika
a large pinch of cayenne pepper

To prepare the red pepper, put it in an ovenproof dish and place under the grill for a *few* minutes. As soon as the top starts to blister and turn black in patches turn it over and grill another side. Keep turning until the entire skin is blistered. Remove from the oven and place in a small dish (not plastic) with a lid so that it can sweat – this loosens the skin. After about 5 minutes, remove the skin and pips and cut the flesh into small squares (15 x 15 mm). Combine the pepper with the remaining ingredients and refrigerate for 1 hour before serving.

FAT AND OIL CONTENT OF ENTIRE DISH
Unsaturated oil – 2 tsp (10 ml)
Saturated fat – may be disregarded

whistleberry salad with sage and onions

In my husband's family, beans are euphemistically referred to as whistleberries. Sounds like something the seven dwarfs would have eaten. After this dish you too may be whistling while you work!

SERVES 2–4 (FOR A CROWD, YOU WILL DEFINITELY NEED TO DOUBLE UP ON QUANTITIES)

1 x 400 g can butter beans (without additives), drained
¼–⅓ small onion, finely chopped (red onion is definitely best)
1 Tbsp (15 ml) finely chopped fresh sage leaves or a sprinkling of dried sage
1 tsp (5 ml) chopped fresh rosemary leaves (optional)
1–2 Tbsp (15–30 ml) Traditional Salad Dressing (page 37)
1 tsp (5 ml) freshly squeezed lemon juice (optional)
herb salt or sea salt
freshly ground black pepper to taste

Combine all the ingredients in a medium-sized bowl.

Set aside for a couple of hours in the refrigerator, turning contents occasionally, to allow the flavours to develop.

FAT AND OIL CONTENT OF ENTIRE SALAD
Unsaturated oil – 1 tsp (5 ml) per tsp of dressing added
Saturated fat – may be disregarded

preserved lemons (page 34)

traditional salad dressing

A good basic dressing that I find pretty hard to beat. When using this dressing with the Raw Energy Salad (page 30) I often make it with lemon juice rather than cider vinegar as lemon juice, despite its sour taste, has an alkalising effect on the digestive system whereas vinegar has an acidic effect. The alkalising effect is more beneficial to the good microflora in the digestive system. The flavour of the cider vinegar may, however, be more to your liking on the other salads.

MAKES ¾ CUP (200 ML)

½ cup + 2 Tbsp (150 ml) cold-pressed sunflower or olive oil (or a combination)
10 tsp (50 ml) lemon juice or cider vinegar
(use less lemon juice if too sour for your palate)
1 tsp (5 ml) herb salt or sea salt to taste
1 tsp (5 ml) mustard powder
1 tsp (5 ml) crushed garlic or 2 cloves garlic, halved
1 Tbsp (15 ml) honey
a grinding of black pepper

Combine all the ingredients in a suitable salad dressing container. The container must be airtight to prevent oxidation of the oil. Shake well before using. Store in the refrigerator.

FAT AND OIL CONTENT IN 1 TSP (5 ML)
Unsaturated oil – 1 tsp (5 ml)
Saturated fat – may be disregarded

home-made garlic mayonnaise

Very addictive, particularly if you like garlic. Self-control will be required! When made with cold-pressed sunflower oil, the mayonnaise has a strong taste of sunflower seeds, which may take a little getting used to. Once mixed with food, however, it is barely noticeable. Olive oil also makes a very strong-flavoured but really delicious mayonnaise – very nice with potato salad.

MAKES 1 CUP (250 ML)

1 large egg
½ tsp (2.5 ml) herb salt or sea salt to taste
½ tsp (2.5 ml) mustard powder
2 Tbsp (30 ml) lemon juice or cider vinegar
2 Tbsp (30 ml) cold-pressed sunflower or olive oil
½–1 tsp (2.5–5 ml) crushed garlic
extra ¾ cup (200 ml) cold-pressed sunflower or olive oil

Blend all the ingredients, except the ¾ cup (200 ml) oil, at high speed in a blender for a few minutes until creamy.

Keep blending while very slowly adding the extra oil in a thin stream. Stop blending when the creamy, thick consistency of mayonnaise is achieved.

Transfer to a container (preferably glass) with a lid, and refrigerate. Keeps well for a few days.

FAT AND OIL CONTENT IN 1 TSP (5 ML)
Unsaturated oil – 1 tsp (5 ml)
Saturated fat – fat in egg may be disregarded if eaten in small quantities

NOTE: I use only 1 egg yolk OR half a blended egg for half the quantity of mayonnaise.

astrid's liver pâté

I have a very creative Swedish friend who does wonderful, rule-breaking things with food. She'll put fresh strawberries with cold chicken pieces and dried banana chips with pasta! This time she put fruit juice with liver, left out the butter and once again produced a winner.

½ large or 1 small onion, chopped
1 large clove garlic, chopped
2 tsp (10 ml) cold-pressed sunflower or olive oil
250 g chicken livers, trimmed
1 large sprig each fresh thyme, oregano, marjoram and rosemary (OR 1 tsp (5 ml) dried mixed herbs)
herb salt or sea salt and freshly ground black pepper to taste
1½ Tbsp (22.5 ml) sherry OR 2–3 Tbsp (30–45 ml) fruit juice (apple, mango or lychee)

Using a pan with a lid, gently fry the onion and garlic in the oil for about 5 minutes.
Add the livers and herbs and cook over a low heat, covered, until the livers are just cooked – don't overcook. Remove the herb sprigs and process the mixture in a food processor until completely smooth. Add seasoning to taste, then add the sherry or fruit juice and blend again.

FAT AND OIL CONTENT OF ENTIRE QUANTITY
Unsaturated oil – 2 tsp (10 ml)
Saturated fat – 3 tsp (15 ml)

NOTE: This pâté freezes well, but the consistency will not be as creamy once defrosted.

roasted red pepper and avocado dip

While devouring a plate of taco chips and roasted red pepper dip, two friends professed a great need to come to my next 'healthy cooking' course. I hastily and surreptitiously read the list of ingredients on the dip bottle and rushed home to attempt a healthy version. I was gratified to see that same look of relish on their faces when they tasted this. Great with Savoury Oat and Sesame Biscuits (page 87), wholemeal bread and salad.

1 large red pepper, charred, peeled and seeded (see method on page 35)
¼ small, ripe tomato
½ tsp (2.5 ml) crushed garlic
½ tsp (2.5 ml) balsamic vinegar or to taste
⅛ tsp hot chilli condiment
a few small leaves from a sprig of fresh oregano
herb salt or sea salt to taste
freshly ground black pepper to taste
2–4 Tbsp (30–60 ml) plain fat-free cottage cheese
½ avocado (use a nice 'creamy' one)
a squeeze of lemon (optional)

Using a food processor, blend the peppers, tomato, garlic, balsamic vinegar, chilli condiment, oregano and seasoning until smooth.
Blend in the cottage cheese and avocado, and adjust seasoning if necessary. If it tastes too 'flat', it may need a drop more balsamic vinegar or a squeeze of lemon.
Transfer to a glass bowl with a lid and refrigerate.

FAT AND OIL CONTENT OF ENTIRE QUANTITY
Unsaturated oil – 2 tsp (10 ml)
Saturated fat – may be disregarded if eaten in moderation

hummus

I'm sure that cheese connoisseurs would be horrified at the comparison, but the first time I tasted this Middle Eastern chickpea spread, it reminded me of cheese! Makes a very tasty spread or an accompaniment to a Raw Energy Salad (page 30).

½ cup (125 ml) dried chickpeas, soaked overnight in
water – should swell to about 1 cup (250 ml)
1 large clove garlic
2 Tbsp (30 ml) tahini
3 Tbsp (45 ml) cold-pressed olive oil
1 Tbsp (15 ml) lemon juice
½–¾ tsp (2.5–4 ml) ground cumin
¼ tsp (1 ml) garam masala or mild curry powder
1 Tbsp (15 ml) chopped fresh parsley (optional)
3–4 Tbsp (45–60 ml) filtered water
herb salt or sea salt to taste
a grinding of black pepper

Boil the soaked chickpeas for 1 about hour (or longer if necessary) until tender – when soft to the bite, they're done! Drain and rinse off any scum with cold water. In a food processor, blend the chickpeas and garlic until fairly smooth, then add all the remaining ingredients, except the water and seasoning, and process until a smooth paste is formed. While blending, add the water 1 Tbsp (15 ml) at a time until you are satisfied with the consistency. Add seasoning. Transfer the hummus to a suitable container and refrigerate.

FAT AND OIL CONTENT OF ENTIRE QUANTITY
Unsaturated oil – 9 tsp (45 ml)
Saturated fat – may be disregarded if eaten in moderation

NOTE: You can omit the olive oil and lemon juice altogether, if desired, and use yoghurt instead for a slightly different taste and a lower fat content. Juggle ingredients until you achieve a taste that pleases you.

quick favourites

bean and basil dip

I've never been a fan of beans so I was most surprised when I really enjoyed this dip, and even more surprised when my four-year-old did too.

1 x 400 g can beans (cannellini, butter beans etc),
drained
1 clove garlic, crushed (optional)
1 Tbsp (15 ml) cold-pressed olive oil
2–3 tsp (10–15 ml) freshly squeezed lemon juice
a small handful of fresh basil leaves
freshly ground black pepper to taste
filtered water to achieve desired consistency

Blend all the ingredients, except the water, in a food processor until smooth. Add water if too dry.

FAT AND OIL CONTENT OF ENTIRE QUANTITY
Unsaturated oil – 3 tsp (15 ml)
Saturated fat – may be disregarded

smoked mackerel, cottage cheese and spring onion dip

Delicious! Double up if expecting guests.

60 g smoked mackerel
4 large sprigs fresh parsley
4 small spring onions, coarsely chopped
5 Tbsp (75 ml) plain fat-free cottage cheese

Blend all the ingredients in a food processor until smooth and creamy.

FAT AND OIL CONTENT OF ENTIRE QUANTITY
Unsaturated oil – 2 tsp (10 ml)
Saturated fat – may be disregarded if eaten in moderation

C A T C H
OF THE DAY

Fish forms an important part of a low-fat diet as it is

very low in saturated fat, but rich in essential fatty acids.

I vividly remember hiding bony pieces of watery hake

under my gem squash as a child, hoping to avoid the

inevitable 'eat it or else' from my dear dad. My husband

introduced me to the pleasures of fresh seafood – what a

difference! Now I'm hooked.

left: fried fish in batter (page 42)

fried fish In batter

The alternative to deep-fried fish doesn't have to be tasteless, watery, steamed fish cooked in foil. Here's how you can make delicious, moist, fried fish in a small quantity of oil. Add a little Cajun spice and you'll want to dine by candlelight!

SERVES 4

600 g fresh firm, white fish fillets
2 handfuls wholemeal or other unrefined flour, spread thickly on a dinner plate
1–2 eggs, beaten in a large, flattish soup bowl
cold-pressed sunflower or olive oil for frying

Using a fork, first dip the fish into the flour to coat it, then dip it into the beaten egg. Set the fish aside on a large plate, ready for frying.

Pour 1–2 tsp (5–10 ml) oil into a frying pan, depending on the size of the pan you're using. I usually manage to fry at least four pieces of fish in a total of 2 tsp (10 ml) oil.

Heat the pan until the oil is hot, then fill the pan with as many pieces of fish as will fit comfortably. As soon as the undersides are golden, add 1 tsp (5 ml) more oil to the pan and turn over the fish. Cook until the other side is golden and a fork slides into the flesh easily. Remove each piece of fish *as soon as* it is cooked or it will dry out. Serve with slices of lemon.

FAT AND OIL CONTENT OF ENTIRE DISH
Unsaturated oil – 1 tsp (5 ml) per tsp oil used for frying
Saturated fat – 1 tsp (5 ml) per egg

IMPORTANT TIPS FOR FRYING: Use pieces of fish that are not too large and not too thick. If the fish is too thick, cut it through the width with a very sharp knife to half the original thickness. If the fillets are quite long, cut them into smaller lengths of about 8–10 cm.

When frying the fish, make sure that the oil is hot enough to make the fish sizzle when you put it in the pan, but not so hot that the oil smokes. Move each piece quickly back and forth *as soon as* it touches the pan so that it doesn't stick to it, then turn the temperature down to low.

strandloper cajun fish spice

Many thanks to Corné at the Strandloper Restaurant for sharing her winning recipe. Store the spice in an airtight container.

¼ cup (60 ml) paprika
2 Tbsp (30 ml) garlic powder
2 Tbsp (30 ml) onion salt
2 Tbsp (30 ml) dried oregano
2 tsp (10 ml) dried rosemary
4 tsp (20 ml) dried thyme
1 tsp (5 ml) white pepper
4 tsp (20 ml) freshly ground black pepper

Sprinkle 1–2 Tbsp (15–30 ml) Cajun spice on a dinner plate. Once the fish pieces have been coated with flour and egg, dip both sides into the spice mix.

You can also use unbattered fish, in which case you can simply sprinkle the spice over the fish using a teaspoon. Set the fish aside, ready for frying.

fish in a creamy sauce

This is always a favourite on my cooking courses – the combination of soy sauce and yoghurt makes a surprisingly superb sauce for the fish. Men can be a bit more difficult to please, however – my brother-in-law's comment was that the chicken was delicious but looked a bit pale!

SERVES 4

1 tsp (5 ml) crushed garlic
2 tsp (10 ml) cold-pressed sunflower or olive oil
600 g firm fish fillets, sliced crossways into 20 mm thick strips
½ tsp (2.5 ml) mild curry powder
2–4 tsp (10–20 ml) MSG-free soy sauce
½ cup + 2 Tbsp (150 ml) plain fat-free yoghurt

Using a medium-sized frying pan, gently fry the garlic in the oil for 30 seconds. Add the fish and curry powder and fry over a medium heat, stirring gently. When the fish is almost cooked, add 2 tsp (10 ml) soy sauce and the yoghurt and cook for 1–2 minutes until the sauce thickens. Add more soy sauce if the sauce tastes too sour and not 'meaty' enough. Remove from the heat. If the sauce becomes very watery, remove the fish with a slotted spoon as soon as it turns white and set aside. Boil the remaining liquid until the sauce thickens, then return the fish to the pan to heat through. Serve on its own or on a bed of brown rice.

FAT AND OIL CONTENT OF ENTIRE DISH
Unsaturated oil – 2 tsp (10 ml)
Saturated fat – may be disregarded

NOTE: For a completely fat-free meal, use the soy sauce in place of the oil to cook the garlic, fish and curry powder.

fish in a creamy sauce

fish pie

This recipe expands on the recipe alongside by adding fried onion, mushrooms and a topping of mashed potato, and turns it into a kind of cottage pie made with fish. It also turns fish for four into fish for six.

Fry 1 large chopped onion and 250 g chopped mushrooms in 2 tsp (10 ml) oil until the onions are tender and the excess liquid has boiled away. Add the fish and cook as in recipe alongside. Transfer the fish mixture to a deep casserole dish. Steam 6 large potatoes and mash with herb salt and a little plain fat-free yoghurt to achieve the desired consistency. Spread the mash over the fish filling and smear 2 tsp (10 ml) Home-made Garlic Mayonnaise (page 37) over the top. Bake at 180 °C (350 °F) until the crust is golden and the filling is bubbling. You may need to grill it for a few minutes.

FAT AND OIL CONTENT OF ENTIRE DISH
Unsaturated oil – 4 tsp (20 ml)
Saturated fat – may be disregarded

spicy thai fish

This is my version of Thai fish. I've never tasted the real thing as I can't eat coconut, but this is what I imagine it must taste like minus the coconut milk. It has a bit of a bite, and is quick, easy and delicious.

SERVES 4

2 tsp (10 ml) cold-pressed sunflower or olive oil
½ tsp (2.5 ml) crushed garlic
½ tsp (2.5 ml) mild curry powder
½ tsp (2.5 ml) sambal oelek chilli (Indonesian relish)
½ tsp (2.5 ml) honey
2 strips lemon grass, cut into 70 mm lengths
½ Tbsp (7.5 ml) finely chopped fresh ginger
600 g fresh firm fish fillets, sliced into 20 mm thick strips
2 tsp (10 ml) MSG-free soy sauce
freshly squeezed lemon juice to taste

Using a medium-sized frying pan, heat the oil to a medium-high temperature. Add the garlic, curry powder, sambal oelek, honey, lemon grass and ginger and fry gently for a few minutes. Add the fish to the spicy oil and, while cooking, sprinkle the soy sauce over the fish. If the sauce becomes too watery, remove the fish with a slotted spoon *as soon as* it turns white and set aside. Boil the remaining liquid until reduced to a thick sauce, then return the fish to the pan to heat through. Add a generous squeeze of lemon juice to the fish pieces and remove from heat immediately. Remove the strips of lemon grass and serve.

FAT AND OIL CONTENT OF ENTIRE DISH
Unsaturated oil – 2 tsp (10 ml)
Saturated fat – may be disregarded

NOTE: I have also cooked calamari rings in the same way and they are delicious!

fish bobotie

I often serve this tasty dish with lightly steamed vegetables and crisp baked potatoes when family come over for an impromptu meal. Hot chutney rounds it off beautifully.

SERVES 4–6

1 large onion, chopped
½ tsp (2.5 ml) crushed garlic
2 tsp (10 ml) cold-pressed sunflower or olive oil
2 tsp (10 ml) mild curry powder
½ tsp (2.5 ml) turmeric
600 g fresh firm, white fish fillets cut into 20 mm thick slices
1 tsp (5 ml) honey
1 Tbsp (15 ml) freshly squeezed lemon juice
¼ cup (60 ml) raisins
1 Tbsp (15 ml) wholemeal flour
herb salt or sea salt and freshly ground black pepper to taste
¾ cup (190 ml) skimmed milk
2 eggs, beaten and mixed into the milk

Preheat the oven to 180 °C (350 °F).

Using a large frying pan with a lid, gently fry the onion and garlic in the oil for a few minutes. Add the curry powder and turmeric, cover and let the mixture sweat over low heat for 10 minutes until the onion is soft. Add a few drops of water if necessary.

Add the fish and cook until just done, then stir in the honey and lemon juice. Transfer the mixture to a medium-sized casserole. Sprinkle the raisins and flour over the fish and add seasoning. Pour the milk and egg mixture over the fish and mix carefully. Bake for about 20 minutes, or until the egg has just set.

FAT AND OIL CONTENT OF ENTIRE DISH
Unsaturated oil – 2 tsp (10 ml)
Saturated fat – 2 tsp (10 ml)

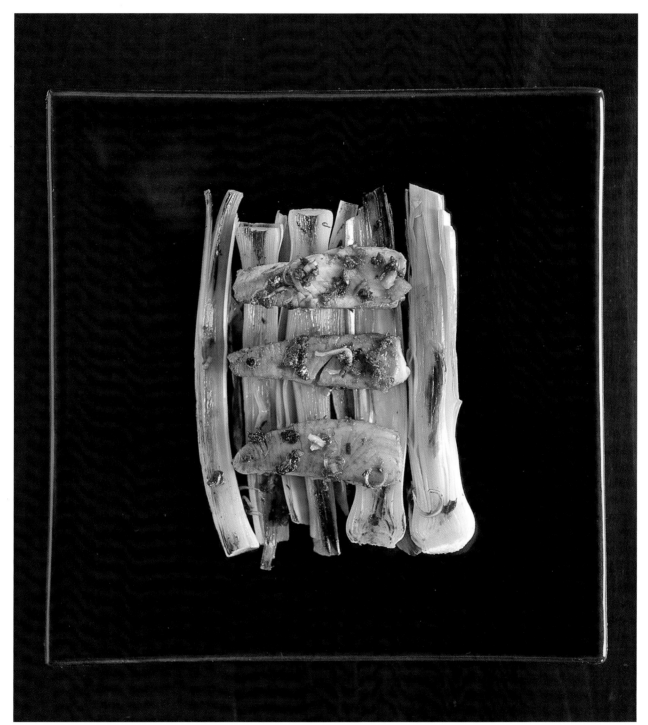

spicy thai fish

haddock with cousous and crisp greens

mediterranean fish casserole

The depth of flavour in this dish belies the simplicity of its preparation. It can be made the day before as the flavour improves by the hour!

SERVES 4

1 large onion, chopped
1 tsp (5 ml) crushed garlic
1 small green pepper, halved, seeded and thinly sliced (omit if you don't like it)
2 tsp (10 ml) cold-pressed olive or sunflower oil
600 g fresh, firm fish fillets, sliced crossways into 20 mm thick strips
18 large kalamata olives, stoned
⅛ tsp fennel seeds
½ cup (125 ml) white or red wine
½ cup (125 ml) tomato passata (no additives)
2 large ripe tomatoes, chopped
2 tsp (10 ml) honey
2 tsp (10 ml) herb salt or sea salt
freshly ground black pepper to taste

Preheat the oven to 180 °C (350 °F).
In a small frying pan with a lid, gently fry the onion, garlic and green pepper in the oil for about 7 minutes.

Arrange the fish pieces in a small casserole and top with the onion, garlic and green pepper mixture. Add the olives, fennel seeds, wine, tomato passata, tomatoes and honey, then bake, uncovered, for about 30 minutes. Season and serve.

FAT AND OIL CONTENT OF ENTIRE DISH
Unsaturated oil – 8 tsp (40 ml)
Saturated fat – may be disregarded if eaten in moderation

haddock with couscous and crisp greens

This is a super-fast, tasty meal to prepare when you really haven't got the energy for the usual meat and three veg.

SERVES 4

1 cup (250 ml) uncooked couscous
1 cup (250 ml) boiling water
400 g haddock fillets
1 tsp (5 ml) mild curry powder
¼ cup (60 ml) chopped spring onion
100 g mangetout, halved
½ cup (125 ml) sweetcorn cut from the cob
1 cup (250 ml) small broccoli florets
2 tsp (10 ml) cold-pressed olive or sunflower oil
2 eggs, hard-boiled and chopped or sliced
lemon slices
herb salt or sea salt to taste
freshly ground black pepper to taste

Place the couscous in a shallow layer in a large casserole dish with a lid. Pour the boiling water over the couscous and cover. When the water has been absorbed, the couscous can be fluffed up with a fork.

In a large frying pan with a lid, poach the haddock fillets in filtered water until cooked. Flake the haddock roughly and set aside. Discard the water.

In the pan, gently stir-fry the curry powder, spring onion, mangetout, sweetcorn and broccoli in the oil for a few minutes only (to retain crispness). Add a little water if necessary to prevent sticking. Stir the couscous, haddock and egg into the vegetables.

Drizzle 2 tsp (10 ml) cold-pressed oil and a squeeze of lemon over each serving just before eating, and season.

FAT AND OIL CONTENT OF ENTIRE DISH
Unsaturated oil – 2 tsp (10 ml) + 1 tsp (5 ml) per tsp oil added

FOWL
PLAY

I have to chuckle when I think of the lean Transkei 'road runner' birds that owe their well-developed thighs to their ability to outrun man and beast. Well, if you can't get hold of any of these then your healthiest option is free-range, corn-fed, farm chickens that 'don't eat their friends for lunch'. If you can find some that have not been given antibiotics, even better. The secret to producing succulent rather than hard, dry chicken breasts (or ostrich fillets) is to slice them across the grain into very thin strips and to cook them until they are just done.

left: aromatic moroccan chicken with couscous (page 52)

chicken breasts in tangy sauce

In what feels like a previous life, my favourite dinner party dish was a delicious pie made with chicken cooked in cream, chutney and soy sauce. Tiddly husbands would say to their wives: 'Darling, you must get this duck recipe!' This is my low-fat alternative, which turned out to be a great favourite and takes a fraction of the time to prepare.

SERVES 4

½ tsp (2.5 ml) crushed garlic
2 tsp (10 ml) cold-pressed sunflower or olive oil
4–5 skinless chicken breast fillets, sliced across the grain into very thin strips
3–4 tsp (15–20 ml) MSG-free soy sauce (the quantity will depend on type of soy sauce used)
1 Tbsp (15 ml) hot chutney
8 Tbsp (120 ml) plain fat-free yoghurt

In a medium-sized frying pan, fry the garlic in the oil for a few seconds, then add the chicken strips. When the chicken starts to sizzle, stir in the soy sauce and chutney. Stir-fry the chicken in the sauce until *nearly* cooked, then add the yoghurt and cook until the chicken is just done.

If the sauce is too watery, remove the chicken with a slotted spoon *as soon as* it is cooked and set aside. Let the excess liquid boil away and the sauce thicken up before replacing the chicken. This will prevent it from becoming overcooked, tough and dry. Serve immediately with baked potatoes and salad or vegetables.

FAT AND OIL CONTENT OF ENTIRE DISH
Unsaturated oil – 2 tsp (10 ml)
Saturated fat – may be disregarded

NOTE: Omit the oil for a lower-fat meal, and cook the garlic and chicken in the soy sauce and chutney from the start.

chicken burgers

Although very low in fat, these burgers are succulent and tasty. Delicious on a wholemeal roll with lettuce, tomato, onion rings and avocado or Home-made Garlic Mayonnaise (page 37).

MAKES 12 SMALL OR 6 MEDIUM BURGERS

½ small onion, roughly chopped
¼ tsp (1 ml) crushed garlic
4 skinless chicken breast fillets, roughly chopped
1 egg
2 large sprigs fresh parsley, chopped
1 large sprig fresh oregano or a pinch of dried oregano
herb salt or sea salt and freshly ground black pepper
Optional, but desirable: 2 tsp (10 ml) chutney and 2 tsp (10 ml) MSG-free soy sauce
cold-pressed sunflower or olive oil for frying

Chop the onion and garlic finely in a food processor. Add the chicken, egg, parsley, oregano, seasoning, chutney and soy sauce (if using), and process until finely chopped.

Heat 1–2 tsp (5–10 ml) oil in a frying pan, and add dessertspoonsful of the mixture into the pan. Fill the pan with as many patties as will fit comfortably – small, flat patties cook through more easily. Reduce the heat and cook the patties until the undersides are golden.

Turn the patties over and cook until the other side is done. If necessary, add 1 tsp (5 ml) more oil to the pan. Make a small incision in one of the burgers to check that it is cooked right through. Remove each burger as soon as it is cooked and serve.

FAT AND OIL CONTENT OF ENTIRE QUANTITY
Unsaturated oil – 1 tsp (5 ml) per tsp oil used for frying
Saturated fat – 1 tsp (5 ml)

NOTE: This also works without the egg, chutney and soy sauce.

chicken burger

aromatic moroccan chicken with couscous

This is an exotic, sweet and savoury tomato-based casserole that tastes good even without the chicken. You can also serve it with Saffron and Chickpea Pilaf (page 69) instead of couscous. Many thanks to Lynn Bedford Hall for the original recipe.

SERVES 4

1 large or 2 small onions, chopped
2 tsp (10 ml) crushed garlic
1 Tbsp (15 ml) finely chopped fresh ginger
2 tsp (10 ml) cold-pressed olive or sunflower oil
½ Tbsp (7.5 ml) cumin seeds
½ tsp (2.5 ml) ground cinnamon
¼ tsp (1 ml) grated nutmeg
2 saffron threads, soaked in 1 tsp (5 ml) water OR
a large pinch of turmeric, if unavailable
4 large ripe tomatoes, chopped
3 large strips lemon peel (20 x 70 mm each)
scant cup (225 ml) pitted prunes
1 cup (250 ml) filtered water
4 skinless chicken breast fillets, sliced across
the grain into thin strips
1 Tbsp (15 ml) MSG-free soy sauce
herb salt or sea salt to taste

couscous

2 tsp (10 ml) cold-pressed olive or sunflower oil
1 Tbsp (15 ml) chopped spring onions
½ tsp (2.5 ml) ground cumin
½ tsp (2.5 ml) ground fennel
¼ tsp (1 ml) ground cinnamon
1½ cups (375 ml) filtered water
6 Tbsp (90 ml) currants or raisins
¼ tsp (1 ml) herb salt or sea salt to taste
1½ cups (375 ml) quick-cooking couscous

Using a large frying pan or pan with a lid, gently fry the onion, garlic and ginger in the oil. After a few minutes, add the cumin seeds, cinnamon, nutmeg, saffron, tomatoes, lemon peel, prunes (break up in the sauce once softened) and water. Simmer for at least 30 minutes, or until the ingredients are cooked through and a thick but juicy sauce has developed.

In a separate small frying pan, cook the chicken strips in the soy sauce until *just* done, then stir the chicken into the tomato and prune sauce. Remove from the heat immediately. Discard the pieces of lemon peel and season with herb salt or sea salt.

To prepare the couscous, use a medium-sized frying pan with a lid, and gently fry the spring onions, cumin, fennel and cinnamon in the oil for a few minutes. Add the water, currants or raisins and herb salt or sea salt and bring to the boil, then add the couscous. Mix well and immediately remove from the heat. Cover the pan with its lid and set aside for 5 minutes, then fluff up the couscous with a fork.

Serve the couscous topped with the tomato, prune and chicken sauce. One or two teaspoons of cold-pressed olive or sunflower oil can also be drizzled over each serving, if desired.

FAT AND OIL CONTENT OF ENTIRE DISH

Unsaturated oil – 4 tsp (20 ml) + 1 tsp (5 ml) per tsp oil added
Saturated fat – may be disregarded

crunchy chicken salad

This is ideal for a summer lunch party. Serve on a bed of crisp lettuce leaves and surround with crunchy raw vegetables. I throw in some crispy baked potatoes and you have a feast!

SERVES 4

250 g white button mushrooms, sliced
4 skinless chicken breast fillets, sliced across the grain into thin strips
¼ tsp (1 ml) mild curry powder
1 Tbsp (15 ml) MSG-free soy sauce
¼ cup (60 ml) Home-made Garlic Mayonnaise (page 37)
8–10 Tbsp (120–150 ml) plain fat-free yoghurt
1–2 Tbsp (15–30 ml) chutney
2–3 sticks celery, thinly sliced crossways (thick white bits discarded)
2 apples, peeled and cut into eight segments each and then thinly sliced
¼ cup (60 ml) raisins
herb salt or sea salt and freshly ground black pepper to taste
salad leaves and other salad ingredients of your choice
4 Tbsp (60 ml) flaked almonds, toasted on a baking sheet at 180 °C (350 °F) until golden

Cook the mushrooms and chicken in a frying pan with the curry powder and soy sauce until the chicken is just done. Transfer to a bowl using a slotted spoon and leave to cool. Let the juices boil away until thick, then add the sauce to the chicken and mushrooms. Add the mayonnaise, yoghurt, chutney, celery, apples and raisins, mix well and season. Pile the chicken salad in the centre of the salad leaves and sprinkle with toasted almonds. Arrange the other salad ingredients around the edge.

FAT AND OIL CONTENT OF ENTIRE DISH
Unsaturated oil – 14 tsp (70 ml)
Saturated fat – may be disregarded if eaten in moderation

chicken with red pepper, tomato and olives

This dish is simple and scrumptious, but takes a solid hour of simmering. It is well worth the wait.

SERVES 4

2 large onions, sliced into eighths
1 tsp (5 ml) crushed garlic
2 red peppers, seeded, quartered and sliced into 20 mm thick strips
2 tsp (10 ml) cold-pressed olive oil
4 ripe tomatoes, cut into eighths
1 Tbsp (15 ml) honey
18 black olives, stoned and quartered
1 cup (250 ml) white wine
herb salt or sea salt and freshly ground black pepper to taste
4 skinless chicken breast fillets, sliced across the grain into very thin strips

Using a large frying pan with a lid, gently fry the onion, garlic and red pepper in the oil for about 5 minutes. Add the tomatoes, honey, olives, wine and seasoning, and fry gently for 15 minutes without the lid. Put the lid back on and simmer for another 45 minutes.

If excess cooking liquid remains at the end of this time, remove the lid and cook over a high heat to reduce the liquid. If the sauce becomes too thick, add a little filtered water.

Stir the chicken strips into the sauce and cook until the chicken is just done. Remove from the heat immediately and set aside for a short time to allow the flavours to develop. Reheat just before serving.

FAT AND OIL CONTENT OF ENTIRE DISH
Unsaturated oil – 8 tsp (40 ml)
Saturated fat – may be disregarded

nasi goreng

asi goreng is an unusual but wonderful Indonesian rice dish traditionally served with a peanut sauce and topped with a fried egg or strips of omelette. When still trying to impress my husband-to-be and his family (strictly 'meat, three veg and gravy' people), I served it without the egg but forgot to explain the peanut sauce. Undaunted by the consistency of the 'gravy', they ladled it generously all over their food. Never before had I seen them eat such delicate portions or leave so early, hence my new, friendlier version, which they love.

SERVES 4–6

1½ cups (375 ml) brown rice
2½ cups (625 ml) filtered water
1 large onion, chopped
1 tsp (5 ml) crushed garlic
2 tsp (10 ml) finely chopped fresh ginger
1 tsp (5 ml) sambal oelek (Indonesian chilli relish)
2 tsp (10 ml) cold-pressed sunflower or olive oil
250 g white button mushrooms, sliced
5 small carrots, julienned
5 courgettes, julienned
4 skinless chicken breast fillets, sliced across the grain into thin strips
a handful of any other vegetables in small pieces (broccoli florets, and so on) (optional)
3 Tbsp (45 ml) ketjap manis (aromatic soy sauce)
3–4 Tbsp (45–60 ml) non-hydrogenated peanut butter mixed with 3 Tbsp (45 ml) water to make a fairly thick sauce
herb salt or sea salt to taste

Bring the rice to the boil in the filtered water, then reduce the heat, cover with a lid and simmer until the rice is tender (not hard, not fluffy). Set aside.

Using a large pot or pan with a lid, gently fry the onion, garlic, ginger and sambal oelek in the oil. After about 5 minutes, add the mushrooms and cook until almost all the mushroom liquid has boiled away.

Increase the temperature to medium-high, add the vegetables and chicken strips and stir-fry until the chicken is *just* done.

If a lot of juice comes out of the vegetables and chicken, remove them with a slotted spoon and let the juice boil away before returning them to the pan. This is to ensure that the vegetables remain crisp.

Remove the pot from heat and stir in the cooked rice (as much as desired), ketjap manis and peanut sauce. Season to taste.

Serve immediately, with 1–2 tsp (5–10 ml) cold-pressed oil added to each serving, if desired.

FAT AND OIL CONTENT OF ENTIRE DISH
Unsaturated oil – 8 tsp (40 ml) + 1 tsp (5 ml) per tsp oil added
Saturated fat – may be disregarded

nasi goreng

chinese-style ostrich fillet

chinese-style ostrich fillet

I didn't have any great success cooking ostrich steak until I decided to think of an ostrich as an overgrown, rather bad-tempered chicken, and treat the meat accordingly. The result was the most succulent, wonderful dish.

SERVES 4

½ tsp (2.5 ml) crushed garlic
1 tsp (5 ml) chopped fresh ginger
1 Tbsp (15 ml) cold-pressed sunflower oil
500 g ostrich fillet, sliced across the grain into very thin slivers
1 Tbsp (15 ml) wholemeal flour
1½ Tbsp (22.5 ml) MSG-free soy sauce
1 Tbsp (15 ml) sherry or grape juice
1 Tbsp (15 ml) cider vinegar
1 Tbsp (15 ml) cold-pressed sesame oil (optional)

In a large frying pan, gently fry the garlic and ginger in the sunflower oil for a few seconds. Add the slivers of fillet and stir-fry over a medium heat. Sprinkle the flour over the meat while cooking. When the meat is only slightly pink in places, transfer to a plate. Pour the soy sauce, sherry or juice, cider vinegar and sesame oil (if using) into the hot pan. Sizzle the mixture to thicken up and then return the fillet to the pan. Toss the strips in the pan until *just* cooked, then remove from heat. Serve immediately.

FAT AND OIL CONTENT OF ENTIRE DISH
Unsaturated oil – 3 tsp (15 ml) + 3 tsp (15 ml) if sesame oil added
Saturated fat – may be disregarded if eaten in moderation

NOTE: If cooking a double portion, cook in two batches of 500 g fillet each. This recipe also works well with slivers of chicken breast or thinly sliced chicken livers. Use 375 g chicken livers for the above quantities and coat the livers with flour before frying.

ostrich fillet stroganoff

My favourite meat dish was always my mom's beef stroganoff. She tried making it for me using ostrich fillet and yoghurt instead of her usual fillet steak and cream – the result was creamy and delicious!

SERVES 4

½ tsp (2.5 ml) paprika
500 g ostrich fillet, sliced across the grain into very thin strips
1 large onion, chopped
1 tsp (5 ml) crushed garlic
2 tsp (10 ml) cold-pressed sunflower or olive oil
250 g white button mushrooms, sliced
¼ cup (60 ml) red wine
1 Tbsp (15 ml) wholemeal flour
½ cup (125 ml) plain fat-free yoghurt
1 tsp (5 ml) MSG-free soy sauce (optional)
herb salt or sea salt and freshly ground black pepper to taste

Sprinkle paprika over the strips of fillet.

In a large frying pan with a lid, fry the onion and garlic in the oil for 5 minutes. Add the mushrooms and fry gently, covered, until the onion is soft and the excess liquid has boiled away (if necessary, remove the lid after a few minutes).

Increase the temperature to medium-high. Add the fillet strips and wine and sprinkle flour over the meat. Stir-fry the fillet for a few minutes until the pink colour is almost gone, then reduce the heat to low. Stir in the yoghurt and soy sauce (if using) and heat through. Remove from the heat and add seasoning. Set aside to allow the flavours to develop. Reheat just before serving.

FAT AND OIL CONTENT OF ENTIRE DISH
Unsaturated oil – 2 tsp (10 ml)
Saturated fat – may be disregarded if eaten in moderation

FROM THE VEGETABLE GARDEN

As an inventive cook, you can be so creative with the vibrant colours and flavours of fresh vegetables. You may even find yourself saying after dessert: 'Oops, we forgot the meat!'

left: scrumptious sweet onion, tomato and olive casserole (page 64)

crispy baked potatoes

My mom added a special something to ordinary baked potatoes by steaming them first, just as you would do for crispy roast potatoes. They have become legendary!

you'll need nothing but potatoes! (do not peel)

Use potatoes that are all about the same size – cut large ones in half if necessary. Steam the potatoes until almost cooked (about 20 minutes). Place the potatoes skin-side down on a non-aluminium baking sheet (no greasing required) and bake at 180 °C (350 °F) for about 1 hour until crisp and golden.
Once the cut sides are crisp, the potatoes can be turned over. Don't turn over before this as the cut side will stick to the baking sheet.
Before serving, cut open and dress each potato with 1 tsp (5 ml) cold-pressed olive or sunflower oil. Alternatively, Home-made Garlic Mayonnaise (page 37) or one of the dips (pages 38–39) can be used.

FAT AND OIL CONTENT
Unsaturated oil – 1 tsp (5 ml) per tsp oil added
Saturated fat – may be disregarded

NOTE: If pressed for time, the steaming can be omitted and the raw potatoes can be pricked and put straight into the oven on a baking sheet and baked until crisp.
For baked potato or squash chips, cut the potatoes and/or squash in half and then into 15 mm thick slices. Do not peel. Arrange the pieces on a baking sheet, skin-side down, and bake until crisp. Dress with oil just before serving.

oven-fried potato chips

When you have the urge for a big greasy plate of 'slap chips' this is where you turn. Don't do it too often, mind!

Cut unpeeled potatoes crossways into 5 mm thick slices and lay in a casserole dish so that they overlap slightly. Drizzle 1 tsp (5 ml) cold-pressed oil per potato over the slices and bake at 180–200 °C (350–400 °F) until crisp and golden. Turn the potatoes over after about 30 minutes to crisp the other side.

FAT AND OIL CONTENT
Unsaturated oil – 1 tsp (5 ml) per tsp oil used
Saturated fat – may be disregarded if eaten in moderation

crispy baked potatoes

potato and squash casserole

This casserole is so packed with vegetables and so full of flavour
that it satisfies even people who love meat and cream.

SERVES 6–8

6 large unpeeled potatoes, sliced into
7.5 mm thick rounds
1 large squash, peeled and sliced into
7.5 mm thick rounds
2 large onions, chopped or sliced
250 g button mushrooms, sliced (optional)
1 Tbsp (15 ml) crushed garlic
a generous sprinkling of chopped fresh
marjoram and rosemary leaves
a generous sprinkling of garlic and herb seasoning,
herb salt or sea salt
2 Tbsp (30 ml) cold-pressed olive or sunflower oil

Preheat the oven to 180 °C (350 °F).
Place the potato and squash slices in a large casserole
with a lid. Mix in the onion, mushrooms (if using),
garlic and herbs. Season and drizzle the oil over
the vegetables. Pour in water to a depth of 5 mm –
there must be *just* enough to ensure that the
vegetables don't burn.
Bake, covered, for 20 minutes, turning occasionally,
then uncover and continue baking for a further
40 minutes, or until the casserole is cooked and all the
water has been absorbed. If the dish dries out too
soon, add a little more water.
One or two teaspoons of cold-pressed olive or
sunflower oil can be added to each serving, if desired.

FAT AND OIL CONTENT OF ENTIRE DISH
Unsaturated oil – 6 tsp (30 ml) + 1 tsp (5 ml) per tsp oil
added
Saturated fat – may be disregarded

fancy baked squash

I often cook a whole squash such as butternut in the oven, it is so
easy and the baking seems to intensify the flavour. One day all
that was on offer at the supermarket were some really tiny baby
butternuts, so I resignedly bought one for each guest and tried to
jolly them up a bit. The result was unexpectedly mouthwatering.

SERVES 6

½–1 very small butternut or other small squash per
person OR
2 large butternuts, halved
2 tsp (10 ml) crushed garlic
2 medium onions, chopped
125 g button mushrooms, sliced
(optional but desirable)
garlic and herb seasoning, herb salt or sea salt to
taste
2 Tbsp (30 ml) cold-pressed olive or sunflower oil

Preheat the oven to 180 °C (350 °F).
Scoop the seeds out of each squash, and arrange the
squash in a large casserole, preferably one with a lid. (I
use two identical shallow roasting tins, one for the bottom and one for the lid.)
On the cut surfaces, spread the garlic, onion and
mushrooms. Season generously and drizzle the oil over
the squash.
Pour a *little* water into the casserole dish to cover the
base – this prevents the pan and any ingredients that
fall off the squash from turning black.
Cover and bake for about 1 hour until the squash
flesh is soft. The lid can be removed for the last
20 minutes of the cooking time.

FAT AND OIL CONTENT OF ENTIRE DISH
Unsaturated oil – 6 tsp (30 ml)
Saturated fat – may be disregarded

baked mediterranean vegetables

Everybody enjoys this colourful dish. It's really simple to make, yet guests are always terribly impressed by it.
The ingredients can be prepared in advance, which is always an advantage when entertaining,
but be sure to leave yourself enough cooking time (about 1 hour) – undercooked aubergines won't do.

SERVES 6

2 aubergines, sliced into 10 mm thick rounds (halve or quarter slices if too large)
250 g white button mushrooms, halved or quartered depending on size
2 large onions, cut into eighths and separated into 'leaves'
5 courgettes, sliced into 20 mm long strips
2 large red and/or yellow peppers, seeded, quartered and sliced into 20 mm thick strips
8–12 baby carrots (optional)
2 tsp (10 ml) crushed garlic OR
1 head of garlic, cloves peeled
3 Tbsp (45 ml) cold-pressed olive or sunflower oil
2 Tbsp (30 ml) balsamic vinegar
12 cherry tomatoes, halved OR
2 tomatoes, cut into eighths
½ Tbsp (7.5 ml) honey, drizzled over the tomatoes
herb salt or sea salt to taste

NOTE: The high oven temperature is crucial for this dish. At a lower temperature the vegetables will merely boil in their own juices and you will end up with a grey, tasteless mush!

Preheat the oven to 220 °C (425 °F).

Place all the vegetables, except the tomatoes, in a huge casserole or a roasting tin – the layer of vegetables must not be too deep. Drizzle the oil and vinegar over the vegetables and toss well.

Bake for about 45 minutes, *turning every 10 minutes* to prevent blackening around the edges. Take care not to break up the vegetables. Add the honeyed tomatoes and continue roasting until the vegetables are tender (about 15 minutes more). Season just before serving.

FAT AND OIL CONTENT OF ENTIRE DISH
Unsaturated oil – 9 tsp (45 ml)
Saturated fat – may be disregarded

mediterranean vegetable casserole

A somewhat different but equally delicious vegetable casserole for four can be prepared with *half* the quantity of aubergines, mushrooms, onion, courgettes, red peppers and garlic above. Add 2 chopped tomatoes, ½ cup (125 ml) tomato passata and 1 tsp (5 ml) honey. Mix in 2 Tbsp (30 ml) finely chopped fresh rosemary and marjoram leaves. Pour over 2 Tbsp (30 ml) cold-pressed olive oil mixed with ½ cup (125 ml) water. Bake, uncovered, at 180 °C (350 °F) for at least 1 hour, or until the ingredients are tender and you have a thick tomato sauce. Add a little water whenever necessary to prevent it boiling dry.

FAT AND OIL CONTENT OF ENTIRE DISH
Unsaturated oil – 6 tsp (30 ml)
Saturated fat – may be disregarded

baked mediterranean vegetables

scrumptious sweet onion, tomato and olive casserole

Onion and tomato tarte tatin is very 'in' at the moment, but on a low-fat diet it is definitely 'out' because the shortcrust pastry pushes the fat content way too high. The filling is the delicious part though, so the pastry can be left out. This also cuts out all the fiddly steps and makes it a quick and easy, but totally delicious, dish to make.

SERVES 4

4 large onions, sliced into 3 thick rings
3 large red tomatoes, quartered
9 kalamata olives, stoned and quartered
4 tsp (20 ml) honey
4 tsp (20 ml) balsamic vinegar
2 tsp (10 ml) cold-pressed olive oil (optional)
a generous sprinkling of garlic and herb seasoning, herb salt OR sea salt
freshly ground black pepper to taste

Preheat the oven to 180 °C (350 °F).
Arrange the thick onion 'circles' in a large casserole (with a lid) so that they don't overlap. Squeeze the tomato quarters into the gaps between the onion rings, and sprinkle the olives over the top. Drizzle the honey, vinegar and oil (if using) over the vegetables and add seasoning.
Bake, covered, for at least 1 hour, or until the onions are soft and sticky. At no stage must the juices start going black as this gives a nasty, bitter taste to the dish. Add a *little* water if necessary to prevent this. The aim is for all the water to have boiled away by the time the onions are soft so that a sticky sauce remains.

FAT AND OIL CONTENT OF ENTIRE DISH
Unsaturated oil – 5 tsp (25 ml)
Saturated fat – may be disregarded

potato, carrot and onion bourguignonne

A very tasty vegetable dish that gives the impression of having meat in it. The flavour definitely improves with time, so it is a good dish to make the day before a dinner party.

SERVES 4

10 carrots (250 g), cut into 10 mm thick slices
4 potatoes, cut into chunks (about 6 pieces each)
2 large onions, cut into eighths
125–250 g button mushrooms, halved
1 tsp (5 ml) crushed garlic
2 tsp (10 ml) cold-pressed sunflower or olive oil
1 Tbsp (15 ml) honey
1 Tbsp (15 ml) tomato purée
3 Tbsp (45 ml) MSG-free soy sauce
⅓ cup + 2 Tbsp (100 ml) red wine
⅓ cup + 2 Tbsp (100 ml) filtered water
1 bay leaf
1 tsp (5 ml) herb salt or sea salt to taste
freshly ground black pepper to taste
½ Tbsp (7.5 ml) cornflour, if required

In a large pan with a lid, gently fry the carrots, potatoes, onions, mushrooms and garlic in the oil. After about 5 minutes, add the honey, tomato purée, soy sauce, wine, water, bay leaf and seasoning.
Boil gently, stirring occasionally, until the sauce is thick and the vegetables are tender. Increase the temperature if necessary or thicken the sauce with cornflour. Add water if too thick.
One or two teaspoons cold-pressed oil may be added to each serving, if desired.

FAT AND OIL CONTENT OF ENTIRE DISH
Unsaturated oil – 2 tsp (10 ml) + 1 tsp (5 ml) per tsp oil added
Saturated fat – may be disregarded

quick favourites

aubergine crisps

SERVES 4

cold-pressed sunflower or olive oil for brushing
2 aubergines, sliced into
10 mm thick rounds

Brush oil on both sides of the aubergine slices and arrange in a large casserole. Salt lightly. Bake at 200 °C (400 °F) for 20–30 minutes, or until the underside is crisp and browned, then bake the other side. Brush with more oil if necessary. The slices are ready when they are crisp and browned on the outside and soft on the inside.

FAT AND OIL CONTENT
Unsaturated oil – 1 tsp (5 ml) per tsp oil used
Saturated fat – may be disregarded if eaten in moderation

aubergine crisps

spicy stir-fried cabbage

SERVES 4

1½ baby cabbages, shredded
¼ tsp (1 ml) crushed garlic
a pinch of curry powder
a dash of MSG-free soy sauce
2 tsp (10 ml) cold-pressed sunflower or olive oil

Stir-fry all the ingredients in the oil for about 10 minutes – the cabbage should be wilted but still crunchy. Serve immediately.

FAT AND OIL CONTENT OF ENTIRE DISH
Unsaturated oil – 2 tsp (10 ml)
Saturated fat – may be disregarded

stir-fried courgettes and tomato

SERVES 4

1 large tomato, chopped
½ tsp (2.5 ml) crushed garlic
6 courgettes, sliced
2 tsp (10 ml) cold-pressed sunflower or olive oil
herb salt or sea salt to taste

Stir-fry all the ingredients in the oil for 20 minutes – the courgettes should retain a little firmness and not be cooked to a pulp. Add seasoning and serve.

FAT AND OIL CONTENT OF ENTIRE DISH
Unsaturated oil – 2 tsp (10 ml)
Saturated fat – may be disregarded

CARBO
LOADING

Pasta, rice and pulses are the staples of many nations, and

you can create endless taste sensations by simply varying

your herbs and spices. Go for brown rice and wholemeal or

rye pasta. This is the one instance when you're allowed

to be 'unrefined'.

left: pasta salad nicoise (page 68)

lemony basil pesto

When I discovered how delicious basil pesto is, I couldn't think why I had waited so long to try it.
Serve mixed into warm pasta and top with sliced avocado and/or salad.

MAKES ½ CUP (125 ML)

1 Tbsp (15 ml) almonds, pecans or hazelnuts
1 cup (250 ml) fresh basil leaves
½ tsp (2.5 ml) crushed garlic
1 tsp (5 ml) herb salt or sea salt to taste
a twist of freshly ground black pepper
⅓ cup (80 ml) cold-pressed olive oil
2 tsp (10 ml) freshly squeezed lemon juice

Using a food processor, chop the nuts very finely until 'powdered'.

Add the basil, garlic, herb salt or sea salt and black pepper and process for a few minutes until the basil leaves are finely chopped. Add the oil and lemon juice and blend until you have a thick green sauce.

FAT AND OIL CONTENT IN 1 TBSP (15 ML) PESTO
Unsaturated oil – 2 tsp (10 ml)
Saturated fat – may be disregarded if eaten in moderation

pasta salad nicoise

This delicious, colourful and light meal needs no accompaniments.

SERVES 4

2 x 170 g cans tuna chunks in brine
150–200 g rosa or cherry tomatoes, halved
12 kalamata olives, stoned and quartered
2 eggs, hard-boiled and cut into eighths
80 g green beans, halved and steamed briefly until bright green and crunchy
2 tsp (10 ml) capers in brine
200 g pasta spirals or other pasta of your choice, cooked until tender, then drained
salad leaves for 4
¼ cup (60 ml) Traditional Salad Dressing (page 37) OR olive oil and balsamic vinegar

Combine all the ingredients, except the salad leaves and dressing, in a large, attractive bowl. Serve the salad leaves in a separate bowl or surround the pasta with the salad leaves on an attractive platter. Pour the salad dressing over the pasta salad and toss gently.

FAT AND OIL CONTENT OF ENTIRE SALAD
Unsaturated oil – 16 tsp (80 ml)
Saturated fat – 2 tsp (10 ml)

chicken spaghetti bolognaise

My children always longed to have spaghetti bolognaise 'like normal people'. I rocketed in their estimation when I realized I could make it with chicken breasts or, even tastier, ostrich fillet.

SERVES 4

1 tsp (5 ml) crushed garlic
1 large onion, chopped
2 tsp (10 ml) cold-pressed olive or sunflower oil
250 g white button mushrooms, sliced
1 x 400 g carton passata (no additives)
1 tsp (5 ml) dried oregano
2 tsp (10 ml) honey
2–3 Tbsp (30–45 ml) MSG-free soy sauce
4–5 skinless chicken breast fillets OR 500 g ostrich fillet (for those with MS), fat removed and finely chopped in food processor
1½ cups (375 ml) filtered water
200 g spaghetti, cooked until tender, then drained
herb salt or sea salt and freshly ground black pepper to taste

In a large frying pan, gently fry the garlic and onion in the oil for 5 minutes. Add the mushrooms, passata, oregano, honey, soy sauce, chicken and water and simmer, covered, for at least 30 minutes. Add seasoning. Serve on a bed of spaghetti or stir the spaghetti into the sauce and serve. A teaspoon or two of cold-pressed oil can be drizzled over each serving, if desired.

FAT AND OIL CONTENT OF ENTIRE DISH
Unsaturated oil – 2 tsp (10 ml) + 1 tsp (5 ml) per tsp oil added
Saturated fat – 1 tsp (5 ml) if using ostrich, otherwise may be disregarded

NOTE: You can omit the oil, if desired, and cook all the ingredients in the tomato purée right from the beginning.

saffron and chickpea pilaf

A spicy, nutty rice dish that's always a hit.

SERVES 6

½ cup (125 ml) uncooked chickpeas, soaked overnight and drained
1 large onion, chopped
1 tsp (5 ml) crushed garlic
½ tsp (2.5 ml) ground cumin
½ tsp (2.5 ml) ground cinnamon
a pinch of turmeric OR 2 threads saffron, soaked in 1 tsp (5 ml) water
1 Tbsp (15 ml) cold-pressed sunflower or olive oil
¾ cup (190 ml) uncooked brown rice, rinsed in cold water and drained
2½ cups (625 ml) filtered water
herb salt or sea salt to taste
¼ cup (60 ml) raisins
freshly ground black pepper to taste
10 almonds, sliced and roasted at 180 °C (350 °F) until golden

Boil the chickpeas for 1 hour, or until tender. Drain.

Using a large frying pan with a lid, gently fry the onion, garlic, cumin, cinnamon and turmeric in the oil for 5 minutes. Add a little water if necessary. Add the rice, water, herb salt or sea salt, raisins and chickpeas. Bring to the boil, then reduce heat and simmer for 20–30 minutes until the rice is cooked and the water has boiled away. Only add more water during cooking if it dries out too soon.

Season with pepper and more salt, if necessary, and top with toasted almonds. A teaspoon or two of cold-pressed oil can be drizzled over each serving, if desired.

FAT AND OIL CONTENT OF ENTIRE DISH
Unsaturated oil – 4 tsp (20 ml) + 1 tsp (5 ml) per tsp oil added
Saturated fat – may be disregarded

pasta with stir-fried vegetables

This is my favourite way of eating pasta. You can prepare this dish using almost any vegetable that you have in your refrigerator. It's tasty and quick to make. You can also serve your stir-fry with rice or couscous.

SERVES 4

1 onion, chopped
½ tsp (2.5 ml) crushed garlic
2 tsp (10 ml) cold-pressed sunflower or olive oil
2–3 Tbsp (30–45 ml) MSG-free soy sauce (optional)
250 g white button mushrooms, sliced
4 courgettes, julienned
3 small carrots, julienned
½ small red pepper, seeded and sliced into thin strips
1 cup (250 ml) small broccoli florets
8 baby sweetcorn, halved
12 mangetout, halved
250 g pasta of your choice, cooked in boiling, salted water until just tender and drained immediately
1 avocado, sliced and dressed with lemon juice (optional)
120 g smoked mackerel, flaked and dressed with lemon juice (optional)

In a large frying pan or wok with a lid, gently fry the onion and garlic in the oil. Alternatively stir-fry them in a little soy sauce.

After a few minutes, add the mushrooms and cook, uncovered, until the juice has nearly boiled away.

Increase the temperature to medium-high and add the vegetables. Stir-fry for a few minutes only. Don't overcook – the vegetables must soften but still be crunchy. Add a dash of soy sauce or a few drops of water if the ingredients stick to the pan. If, at any stage, you end up with too much liquid, remove the vegetables with a slotted spoon and set aside. Let juice boil away and thicken before returning the vegetables to the pan – they must be stir-fried not boiled.

Add the cooked pasta a spoon at a time until the desired ratio of pasta to vegetables is obtained, and toss to mix.

Serve immediately. Add 1–2 tsp (5–10 ml) pesto or cold-pressed oil and/or a sprinkling of soy sauce to each serving, if desired. Top with avocado slices and/or smoked mackerel (if using).

FAT AND OIL CONTENT OF ENTIRE DISH
Unsaturated oil in oil – 2 tsp (10 ml) + 1 tsp (5 ml) per tsp oil added
See pesto recipe (page 68) and List 1 (page 13) for pesto, avocado and mackerel fat quantities
Saturated fat – may be disregarded if eaten in moderation (Those with MS should not use pesto, avocado and mackerel together as the combination will be too high in saturated fat.)

pasta with stir-fried vegetables

rice with squash, lentils and a spicy peanut flavour

curried rice and spinach

This is an unsophisticated but very satisfying lunch for a winter's day. I often give this to my children instead of *more* bread when they come home from school.

SERVES 3–4

1 cup (250 ml) uncooked brown rice, rinsed in cold water and drained
2 cups (500 ml) filtered water
½ tsp (2.5 ml) mild curry powder
½ large tomato, chopped
a large handful well-washed spinach leaves, stalks removed
½ cup (125 ml) sweetcorn kernels
cold-pressed sunflower or olive oil
herb salt or sea salt to taste

Using a medium-sized pot with a lid, boil the rice, curry powder and chopped tomato in the water (with the lid off and over a high heat). When the water has evaporated to the point where it just covers the rice, add the spinach.

Reduce the heat and simmer with the lid on until the water has almost boiled away – the mixture should almost be cooked by this stage. If not, add a *little* water and cook for a while longer. Lastly, stir the corn kernels into the rice mixture and continue cooking until all the water has boiled away.

Run a blunt knife through the dish to chop up the cooked spinach. Add 1–2 tsp (5–10 ml) oil and a sprinkling of herb salt or sea salt to each serving just before eating.

FAT AND OIL CONTENT IN 1 SERVING
Unsaturated oil – 1 tsp (5 ml) per tsp oil added
Saturated fat – may be disregarded

rice with squash, lentils and a spicy peanut flavour

In this dish the lentils add a pleasant nuttiness without being the dominant flavour. Remember to check the lentils for stones.

SERVES AT LEAST 6

½ cup (125 ml) uncooked green lentils
2 medium onions, chopped
1 tsp (5 ml) crushed garlic
1 Tbsp (15 ml) very finely chopped fresh ginger
1 Tbsp (15 ml) cold-pressed sunflower or olive oil
600 g squash, peeled and cut into 20 mm thick cubes
½ Tbsp (7.5 ml) mild curry powder
½ tsp (2.5 ml) garam masala
1 tsp (5 ml) sambal oelek (Indonesian chilli relish)
2½ cups (625 ml) cooked brown rice
2 Tbsp (30 ml) non-hydrogenated peanut butter or tahini
¼ cup (60 ml) hot water (omit if using tahini)
2 Tbsp (30 ml) ketjap manis (sweet soy sauce)
herb salt or sea salt to taste

Rinse the lentils under cold water and boil for about 20 minutes until just tender.

In a large pot with a lid, gently fry the onion, garlic and ginger in the oil for a few minutes, stirring regularly. Add the squash, curry powder, garam masala and sambal oelek and simmer, covered, until the squash is tender. Add a little water, if necessary, to prevent sticking. Stir in the cooked rice and lentils and set aside.

In a cup, mix the peanut butter and hot water until smooth, then stir this sauce (or tahini), the sweet soy sauce and herb salt into the squash-lentil mixture.

FAT AND OIL CONTENT OF ENTIRE DISH
Unsaturated oil – 6 tsp (30 ml) + 1 tsp (5 ml) per tsp oil added
Saturated fat – may be disregarded

ideas with rice

Cook 1 cup (250 ml) brown rice and then mix in the combination of your choice. Serve with a salad and you'll have a healthy meal for 4.

apple and mushrooms with a hint of curry

2 apples, peeled, cored and chopped
1 medium onion, chopped
½ tsp (2.5 ml) crushed garlic
2 tsp (10 ml) cold-pressed sunflower or olive oil
125 g white button mushrooms, sliced
3 Tbsp (45 ml) sultanas or currants
2 tsp (10 ml) mild curry powder
9 kalamata olives, stoned and quartered AND/OR
6 stuffed green olives, sliced
herb salt or sea salt and freshly ground
black pepper to taste
4 Tbsp (60 ml) flaked almonds, toasted at 180 °C
(350 °F) until golden

In a large frying pan with a lid, gently fry the apples, onion and garlic in the oil for a few minutes until the onion is translucent. Stir regularly to prevent sticking. Add the mushrooms, sultanas and curry powder and fry until the excess liquid from the mushrooms has boiled away. Stir the cooked rice and olives into the pan and add seasoning.

Sprinkle the toasted almonds over the top and serve warm with 1–2 tsp (5–10 ml) cold-pressed olive or sunflower oil drizzled over each serving.

FAT AND OIL CONTENT OF ENTIRE DISH

**Unsaturated oil – 8 tsp (40 ml) + 1 tsp (5 ml)
per tsp oil added
Saturated fat – may be disregarded**

mangetout, sweetcorn and yellow pepper

1 large onion, chopped
½ tsp (2.5 ml) crushed garlic
2 tsp (10 ml) cold-pressed sunflower or olive oil
½ tsp (2.5 ml) paprika
1 sprig fresh oregano, chopped
2 sprigs fresh thyme
½ large yellow or red pepper, seeded and sliced
70 g mangetout, halved
½ cup (125 ml) sweetcorn kernels

In a large frying pan, gently fry the onion and garlic in the oil for about 5 minutes, stirring. Add a few drops of water if necessary. Add paprika, oregano, thyme and pepper and cook, covered, over low heat until the onion is translucent. Stir in the mangetout and sweetcorn and fry, uncovered, for a few minutes to soften them slightly.

FAT AND OIL CONTENT OF ENTIRE DISH

**Unsaturated oil – 2 tsp (10 ml) + 1 tsp (5 ml) per tsp oil added
Saturated fat – may be disregarded**

thyme and garlic

8 tsp (40 ml) cold-pressed olive or sunflower oil
1–2 cloves garlic, crushed
1 Tbsp (15 ml) fresh thyme, stalks removed

Pour the oil into a cup and add the garlic and thyme so that the flavours can mingle. Stir the mixture into cooked rice and stir-fry for 1–2 minutes. Serve hot.

FAT AND OIL CONTENT OF ENTIRE DISH

**Unsaturated oil – 8 tsp (40 ml)
Saturated fat – may be disregarded**

savoury rice with avocado and prawns

Every year, in prawn season, my husband and eldest daughter disappear for hours up the Kowie River to net the most delicious, sweet, fresh prawns. We toss the prawns around a hot pan for a few minutes until just pink and then eat them with Home-made Garlic Mayonnaise (page 37) and lemon juice. This dish is what I usually prepare when we want to make a meal of it. The rice is also delicious without the prawns and avocado.

SERVES 4–6

rice
1 cup (250 ml) uncooked brown rice, rinsed in cold water and drained
½ tsp (2.5 ml) mild curry powder
2 cups (500 ml) filtered water
2 tsp (10 ml) cold-pressed sunflower or olive oil
1 large onion, chopped
1 tsp (5 ml) crushed garlic
1 large tomato, chopped
250 g white button mushrooms, sliced
4–6 courgettes, julienned
½ red or yellow pepper, seeded and sliced into strips
herb salt or sea salt and freshly ground black pepper to taste

prawn and avocado topping
±50 prawns (or whatever you have available), peeled and defrosted
¼ tsp (1 ml) crushed garlic
2 tsp (10 ml) cold-pressed sunflower or olive oil
freshly squeezed lemon juice
herb salt or sea salt to taste
1 avocado, sliced and dressed with lemon juice

Bring the rice and curry powder to the boil in the filtered water, then reduce heat, cover with a lid and simmer until the rice is tender (not hard, not fluffy).

In a large frying pan with a lid, gently fry the onion and garlic in the oil for about 5 minutes. Add a few drops of water if necessary. Add the tomato and mushrooms and fry until the excess liquid has boiled away. Cook, uncovered, if there is too much liquid in the pan.

Add the courgettes and peppers and stir-fry over medium heat for about 10 minutes. Remove from heat while the courgettes are still firm as they will soften further due to the heat of the dish. Stir the cooked rice into the vegetables and add seasoning. Transfer the mixture to a serving dish and keep warm.

Fry the prawns and garlic in the oil until the prawns are *just* pink, then remove from heat immediately. If using bought prawns, you virtually only have to warm them up. Squeeze a generous amount of lemon juice over the prawns and season with Herbamare or sea salt.

Arrange the prawns and avocado slices on top of the rice and vegetable mixture and serve. One or two teaspoons cold-pressed oil can be drizzled over each serving, if desired. Home-made Garlic Mayonnaise (page 37) is also delicious with this dish.

FAT AND OIL CONTENT OF ENTIRE DISH
Unsaturated oil – 8 tsp (40 ml) + 1 tsp (5 ml)
per tsp oil added
Saturated fat – may be disregarded if eaten in moderation

JUST
DESSERTS

Say goodbye to guilt! A wholefood

diet includes sweet treats that

have nutritional value and are

not full of all the empty calories

and toxins of junk food. But let

moderation be your guide.

**left: cottage cheese
cassata (page 80)**

banana ambrosia

This is a deliciously sticky, nutty pudding that you may enjoy even if you're not particularly fond of bananas.

SERVES 4

6 bananas, halved lengthways
2 Tbsp (30 ml) honey
4 Tbsp (60 ml) nuts, chopped (almonds, pecans, hazelnuts, etc)
2 Tbsp (30 ml) sunflower seeds
3 Tbsp (45 ml) pure orange juice or sherry
plain fat-free yoghurt

Arrange the bananas in a single layer in a medium-sized baking dish (about 20 x 30 cm). Drizzle the honey over the bananas, and sprinkle the chopped nuts and sunflower seeds over the top. Pour the juice into the dish to prevent sticking and burning, and bake at 200 °C (400 °F) for 20–30 minutes, until golden and sticky. Baste occasionally. Serve warm with plain fat-free yoghurt.

FAT AND OIL CONTENT OF ENTIRE DISH
Unsaturated oil – 5 tsp (25 ml)
Saturated fat – may be disregarded

apple crumble

A simple, wholesome, everyday kind of dessert that children (and adults) love!

SERVES 4

4 apples, peeled and chopped
10 large dates, chopped
1 Tbsp (15 ml) honey
½ cup (125 ml) filtered water
¼ tsp (1 ml) ground cinnamon
¼ tsp (1 ml) vanilla extract
½ cup (125 ml) Granola (page 16)
4 Tbsp (60 ml) pecans, chopped

home-made custard
1 egg yolk
¾ cup + 2 Tbsp (200 ml) plain fat-free yoghurt
2 Tbsp (30 ml) honey
½ tsp (2.5 ml) vanilla extract

Place the apple, dates, honey, water, cinnamon and vanilla extract in a medium-sized pan with a lid. Bring to the boil, reduce heat and simmer for 20 minutes until the apple mixture is soft and looks puréed.

Spoon the mixture into individual bowls. Top with a layer of granola and chopped nuts and serve warm with home-made custard.

To make the custard, whisk all the ingredients together in a pan. Heat gently, stirring regularly, until thickened (about 15 minutes).

FAT AND OIL CONTENT OF ENTIRE DISH
Unsaturated oil – 4 tsp (20 ml)
Saturated fat – 1 tsp (5 ml) in custard

apple crumble

cottage cheese cassata

This is a really delicious pudding, packed with nuts and fruit and suitable for dinner parties. The wonderfully creamy texture belies the low-fat content. Feel free to vary the fruit and nuts to suit your own palate.

SERVES 4–8

1 x 250 g tub plain fat-free cottage cheese, sieved
1 tsp (5 ml) very finely chopped fresh ginger (optional)
1 Tbsp (15 ml) grated lemon peel
25 g pecans, coarsely chopped
3 Tbsp (45 ml) hazelnuts, roasted at 180 °C (350 °F) until golden, and coarsely chopped
4 Tbsp (60 ml) almonds, roasted at 180 °C (350 °F) until golden, and coarsely chopped
4 Tbsp (60 ml) dried apricots, finely chopped
4 Tbsp (60 ml) dried figs, finely chopped
4 Tbsp (60 ml) raisins OR chopped dates
1 Tbsp (15 ml) honey, or to taste
½ tsp (2.5 ml) freshly squeezed lemon juice (optional)

In a mixing bowl, combine the cottage cheese, ginger (if using), lemon peel, nuts, chopped fruit and honey. Add lemon juice, if desired. Transfer the mixture to a small dish (about 12 cm diameter) and freeze. Cut into 8 thin slices and serve frozen.

FAT AND OIL CONTENT OF ENTIRE DISH
Unsaturated oil – 8 tsp (40 ml)
Saturated fat – may be disregarded if eaten in moderation

spicy peach cake

This is an adaptation of an old favourite – apple cake with rich sauce poured over it – but this one you can eat without blowing your diet. You can also use pear or apple slices, if preferred.

SERVES 6–8

1 x 410 g can sliced peaches in fruit juice (not syrup), juice reserved
1 Tbsp (15 ml) cold-pressed sunflower oil
¼ cup (60 ml) reserved juice from the canned peaches plus 3-4 Tbsp (45-60 ml) for spooning
¼ cup (60 ml) honey
1 egg
½ cup (125 ml) wholemeal flour
¼ tsp (1 ml) salt
¼ tsp (1 ml) cinnamon
½ tsp (2.5 ml) bicarbonate of soda
6 Tbsp (90 ml) pecan nuts, chopped

Preheat the oven to 180 °C (350 °F).

In a bowl, whisk together the oil, juice, honey and egg, then mix in the flour, salt, cinnamon and bicarbonate of soda.

Pour the mixture into a 20 cm diameter pie dish. (Don't be concerned about the small quantity of batter.) Arrange the peach slices on top. Sprinkle over the chopped pecans.

Bake for about 20 minutes, or until a skewer comes out clean.

Spoon the extra peach juice over the cake and return to switched off oven for 10 minutes. Serve warm with a dollop of plain fat-free yoghurt, if desired.

FAT AND OIL CONTENT OF ENTIRE DISH
Unsaturated oil – 8 tsp (40 ml) – eat in moderation
Saturated fat – 1 tsp (5 ml)

light lemon mousse tart

This tastes a little like lemon meringue without the meringue. It's not overly sweet, has a lovely, fresh taste, and is very low in fat. You can also omit the base and prepare it as a mousse.

SERVES 2 (DOUBLE OR TREBLE FOR A BIGGER TART)

tart base (optional)
10 almonds or other nuts of your choice
⅓ cup + 2 Tbsp (100 ml) oats
8 dates
¼ tsp (1 ml) ground ginger (optional)

filling
1 large egg yolk
¾ + 2 Tbsp (200 ml) plain fat-free yoghurt
2 Tbsp (30 ml) honey
peel of ½ lemon, cut into large pieces (use peel of 1 lemon for tripled quantities)
1 tsp (5 ml) gelatine

To prepare the base, process the nuts in a food processor until powdered. Add the remaining ingredients and process until finely chopped. Add a *few* drops of water to bind the mixture and press into a dish (12 cm diameter). For the filling, place the egg yolk, yoghurt and honey in a heavy-bottomed pot and whisk together. Add the lemon peel. Heat slowly until bubbling gently – keep stirring. Cook for 10–15 minutes until the raw egg taste has gone and there is a strong lemon flavour to the mixture. Don't let it boil or it will curdle! Discard the lemon peel. In a cup, dissolve the gelatine in 2 Tbsp (30 ml) boiling water. Stir the gelatine into the filling mixture, and remove from heat. Pour the filling over the base and refrigerate until set.

FAT AND OIL CONTENT OF ENTIRE DISH
Unsaturated oil (in base) – 1 tsp (5 ml)
Saturated fat – 1 tsp (5 ml)

date, nut and brandy pudding

The traditional version can be very sweet and rich. This is a much milder and very low-fat version.

SERVES 6–8

cake
125 g dates, stoned
½ cup (125 ml) boiling water
¾ cup (190 ml) wholemeal flour
½ tsp (2.5 ml) bicarbonate of soda
¼ cup (52.5 ml) pecans, chopped
2 Tbsp (30 ml) honey
1 egg, beaten

sauce
½ cup (125 ml) filtered water
1 Tbsp (15 ml) honey
½ tsp (2.5 ml) vanilla extract
2 Tbsp (30 ml) brandy

Preheat the oven to 180 °C (350 °F).

Soak the dates in the boiling water until cool, then purée the dates and water in a food processor.

In a mixing bowl, combine the flour, bicarbonate of soda and nuts. Add the date purée, honey and egg and mix well. Pour the mixture into a small baking dish (about 20 x 20 cm) and bake for 20–30 minutes, or until a knife comes out clean.

To make the sauce, mix together the water, honey and vanilla extract in a small pan. Bring to the boil to dissolve the honey, then remove from heat. Stir in the brandy and pour the sauce over the cake. Return to the switched off oven for 5–10 minutes.

Serve warm with plain fat-free yoghurt, if desired.

FAT AND OIL CONTENT OF ENTIRE DISH
Unsaturated oil – 6 tsp (30 ml) – eat in moderation
Saturated fat – 1 tsp (5 ml)

moist apple and hazelnut tart

It's hard to believe that a tart recipe without flour will work, but it does, beautifully – perfect for those trying to avoid wheat. It does contain rather a lot of honey, but as long as you don't eat half the tart it shouldn't be too bad for you. It really is worth making and is always pounced upon at dinner parties.

MAKES 8–12 SLICES

100 g hazelnuts, roasted at 180 °C (350 °F) until golden
3 large eggs, separated
½ cup (125 ml) honey
1 large crisp green apple, peeled and grated

Rub the roasted hazelnuts in a teatowel to loosen the skins, then chop the nuts very finely in a food processor. In a bowl, whisk together the egg yolks and honey until smooth, then stir in the nuts and apple. Whisk the egg whites until soft peaks form, then fold gently into the above mixture. Pour into a pie dish (20 cm diameter) and bake at 180 °C (350 °F) for about 30 minutes, or until a skewer comes out clean. Leave to cool and serve with a dollop of plain fat-free yoghurt, if desired.

FAT AND OIL CONTENT OF ENTIRE DISH
Unsaturated oil – 10 tsp (50 ml) – eat in moderation
Saturated fat – 3 tsp (15 ml)

children's treats

frozen banana ice cream

Blend 1 banana with 1–2 tsp (5–10 ml) carob powder and freeze.

fruit juice jelly

To 1 cup (250 ml) pure fruit juice add 2 tsp (10 ml) gelatine dissolved in 2 Tbsp (30 ml) boiling water. Stir well and refrigerate until set.

fruit lollies

Freeze pure fruit juice in plastic lolly moulds.

nutty crunch

Heat 2 Tbsp (30 ml) raw honey in a pan until bubbling gently. Add as many chopped nuts and/or sunflower and sesame seeds as the honey will coat. Stir over a medium heat until the nuts are golden. Spread in a layer on baking paper and refrigerate to harden.

carob and rice balls

Process 4 rice cakes (8 cm diameter x 1 cm thick) until coarsely chopped. In a small pan, combine 3 Tbsp (45 ml) cold-pressed sunflower oil, 3 Tbsp (45 ml) carob powder and 3 Tbsp (45 ml) honey. Heat gently, then stir in the rice cake crumbs. Put teaspoonfuls in very small paper cupcake holders. Refrigerate. Makes 12.

carob and nut truffles

Process ½ cup (125 ml) rolled oats, ½ cup (125 ml) nuts, 10 dates and ¼ cup (60 ml) carob powder in a food processor until almost smooth. Add 3–4 Tbsp (45–60 ml) water slowly, while blending, until the mixture sticks together easily without becoming too sloppy. Roll into small balls or press the mixture into a small dish and cut into 12 squares. Refrigerate.

NOTE: Refer to page 13 for fat and oil content.

nutty crunch

FRESH FROM THE OVEN

Fractious children are transformed into little angels when their

home-coming is sweetened by the sight and smells of freshly baked

goodies. My brother had prospective buyers fighting over his minute

London flat on the strength of the aroma of baking bread wafting

down the stairs.

left: rich fruit cake (page 91)

home-made wholemeal bread

A friend transformed my infamous home-made wholemeal 'brick' into the simplest, most addictive loaf by cutting out the kneading and adding more water. Try it.

MAKES 1 LOAF

500 g (about 4 cups) wholemeal flour
2 tsp (10 ml) instant yeast
1 tsp (5 ml) herb salt or sea salt to taste
1 Tbsp (15 ml) honey
2½ cups (625 ml) tepid water
¼–½ cup (60–125 ml) sunflower seeds AND/OR
2 Tbsp (30 ml) poppy seeds (optional)
a handful of raisins (optional)
seeds for sprinkling on top of the loaf (sesame, sunflower, pumpkin, poppy) (optional)

VERY IMPORTANT NOTE: Flours can vary in the quantity of water that they will absorb. Add the additional water slowly until there is *just* enough water to moisten all the flour. You should be able to stir the flour into the water easily without having to work too hard at it – but you don't need a drop more water than this. It should be too wet to knead but not runny enough to pour. Too much water will result in a loaf that never dries out no matter how long it cooks. If your oven does not have a warming drawer, let the bread rise on the lowest setting (less than 100 °C/200 °F) and when ready for baking, turn the oven up to 180 °C (350 °F). Bake for about 5 minutes longer to take the heating time into account.

Switch on the warming drawer.

Oil a bread tin with cold-pressed oil and sprinkle with flour until all sides are coated. Discard excess.

In a large mixing bowl, mix the yeast into the flour, then mix in the salt and honey. Add 2 cups (500 ml) tepid water and mix well. Add the remaining water slowly, stopping when desired consistency is reached (see note alongside).

Put the dough into the tin and leave to rise in the warming drawer for 25–30 minutes, until doubled in size. (Don't let it over-rise because then it actually starts deflating again. I find that if I catch it when it could rise just a fraction more, it rises a little more while cooking.) In the meantime, preheat the oven to 200 °C (400 °F).

When the dough has doubled in size, transfer to the oven and bake for 30 minutes, or until the crust is golden and makes a hollow sound when tapped. If the crust is not golden after 30 minutes, increase the oven temperature and bake a bit longer. Turn out onto a cooling rack when done.

This bread lasts well for quite a few days without drying out. In very hot weather, the yeast tends to go sour after a day so it is best kept in the refrigerator. Any bread that is not eaten the same day can be sliced and put into the freezer and defrosted when required.

FAT AND OIL CONTENT
Unsaturated oil – 1 tsp (5 ml) per 1 Tbsp (15 ml) seeds
Saturated fat – may be disregarded

gluten-free bread

The thought of having to give up wheat fills most people with horror as a bleak, breadless future is imagined. Never fear – here is something that should fill the gap very nicely. This loaf contains no wheat, dairy products or eggs – but it does contain an amazing natural substance called guar gum, which is available in healthfood shops and without which your bread would probably fall apart.

MAKES 1 LOAF

2 cups (2 x 250 ml) gluten-free high fibre bread flour
2 cups (2 x 250 ml) gluten-free flour
1 tsp (5 ml) bicarbonate of soda
1 tsp (5 ml) guar gum
1 Tbsp (15 ml) honey
¼ cup (60 ml) cold-pressed olive or sunflower oil
1 large crisp green apple, grated
1 cup (250 ml) carrot pulp (the part that remains after juice has been extracted) (optional)
±1½ cups (325 ml) filtered water

Preheat the oven to 180 °C (350 °F). Oil a bread tin (non-aluminium) and coat with gluten-free flour. Combine all the ingredients, except the water, in a large mixing bowl. Add just enough water to moisten all the flour. Don't add any more water than is necessary otherwise you'll end up with a loaf that never dries out.
Spoon the dough into the bread tin and bake for 45 minutes, or until a skewer comes out clean.

FAT AND OIL CONTENT OF ENTIRE LOAF
Unsaturated oil – 12 tsp (60 ml) – about 1 tsp (5 ml) per slice
Saturated fat – may be disregarded if eaten in moderation

savoury oat and sesame biscuits

On my first cooking course I produced an impressive selection of new dips and spreads. These biscuits were hastily invented after it was pointed out to me that there was nothing to dip into the dips!

MAKES 16 BISCUITS

2 cups (500 ml) raw rolled oats
½ tsp (2.5 ml) herb salt or sea salt
a large pinch of bicarbonate of soda
2 Tbsp (30 ml) cold-pressed olive or sunflower oil
2 Tbsp (30 ml) sesame seeds

Preheat the oven to 200 °C (400 °F).
Process all the ingredients in a food processor until fairly finely chopped. Keep blending while adding water by the tablespoon, stopping when there is *just* enough water to make the mixture stick together easily when pinched between your fingers (when it is no longer dry and crumbly).
On your work surface, roll out the dough into two rounds (about 4 mm thick and 18 cm in diameter). Using a plate as a template, cut each into a circle, then cut each circle into 8 triangular sections. Use a blunt knife to lift each section off the work surface.
Arrange on a baking sheet (no oiling required) and bake for 20–25 minutes until crisp and golden. Turn the biscuits over halfway through the cooking time.
Turn out onto a cooling rack when done.

FAT AND OIL CONTENT PER BISCUIT
Unsaturated oil – ½ tsp (2.5 ml)
Saturated fat – may be disregarded if eaten in moderation

NOTE: For sweet carob and nut biscuits, add 16 chopped dates, 4 Tbsp (60 ml) carob powder, 60 g chopped pecans and 2 Tbsp (30 ml) honey. Proceed as above.

divine olive foccacia

For years I tried in vain to make a low-fat version of one of those delectable looking foccacias that you see in the shops. Then the idea for this strange combination of ingredients popped into my mind, and it works – must have been divine inspiration! It is moist enough to require no additional oil, but a drizzle of olive oil never goes amiss.

MAKES 12 SMALL SLICES

1½ crisp green apples, grated
(makes ¾ cup)
3 small courgettes, grated
(makes ¾ cup)
⅓ cup (80 ml) finely chopped onion
1½ cups (325 ml) wholemeal flour
½ Tbsp (7.5 ml) instant yeast
1 tsp (5 ml) honey
1 tsp (5 ml) herb salt or sea salt
1 egg, beaten
½ cup (125 ml) tepid water
18 large kalamata olives, stoned and quartered
1 Tbsp (15 ml) fresh rosemary leaves
1 Tbsp (15 ml) fresh thyme leaves
herb salt or coarse sea salt for sprinkling on top

Preheat the oven to 200 °C (400 °F).

Combine the apple, courgettes, onion, flour, yeast, honey, herb salt or sea salt and egg in a mixing bowl. Stir in just enough of the water to bind all the dry ingredients. Don't make it too wet.

Oil the base of a large baking dish (about 20 x 30 cm) and coat with flour. Carefully spread the mixture in a thin layer (10–15 mm thick) over the base of the dish, taking care not to remove the flour coating. Place the dish in a warm place for 10 minutes to allow the mixture to rise while you prepare the olives and herbs.

Sprinkle the olives and herbs evenly over the top and gently push them into the dough, then cut diagonal slits in the top of the dough to make a grid pattern. Sprinkle with herb salt or coarse sea salt, then return to the warm place for 10–15 minutes, or until it has doubled in size.

Place in the oven and bake for 15 minutes, or until a skewer comes out clean.

Eat while still warm. One or two tablespoons of cold-pressed olive or sunflower oil can be drizzled over the foccacia, if desired.

FAT AND OIL CONTENT OF ENTIRE LOAF
Unsaturated oil – 6 tsp (30 ml) + 1 tsp (5 ml)
per tsp oil added
Saturated fat – 1 tsp (5 g) – eat in moderation

divine olive foccacia

ginger muffins with lemon frosting

If you like fresh ginger, you'll love these muffins. On my cooking courses, people thought the lemon frosting
was an alternative to cream and they put great dollops of it with everything and ate it with relish –
so I guess it has more applications than I realized.

MAKES 12 MEDIUM-SIZED MUFFINS

muffins

2 Tbsp (30 ml) peeled and coarsely chopped
fresh ginger
3 crisp green apples,
peeled and quartered
½ cup (125 ml) dates
1 Tbsp (15 ml) freshly squeezed lemon juice
¼ cup (60 ml) cold-pressed sunflower oil
¼ cup (60 ml) honey
1 large egg
1½ cups (325 ml) wholemeal flour
¼ tsp (1 ml) salt
½ tsp (2.5 ml) bicarbonate of soda
4 tsp (20 ml) pecans, chopped, for decorating
(optional)

lemon frosting (optional)

1 x 250 g tub plain fat-free cottage cheese, sieved
½ Tbsp (7.5 ml) finely grated lemon zest
2 Tbsp (30 ml) honey

Preheat the oven to 180 °C (350 °F) and oil a muffin tin.

In a food processor, chop the ginger, apples and dates until well 'puréed'. Transfer to a mixing bowl and add the lemon juice, oil, honey and egg, followed by the flour, salt and bicarbonate of soda. Stir to combine the ingredients, but don't overmix – the mixture should still be lumpy.

Spoon the mixture into the muffin tin and bake for 20–25 minutes, or until a skewer comes out clean. Turn out onto a wire rack to cool.

To make the lemon frosting, combine all the ingredients in a small bowl and mix well. Refrigerate.

When the muffins have cooled completely, glaze with lemon frosting and sprinkle with chopped pecans.

FAT AND OIL CONTENT

Unsaturated oil per muffin – 1 tsp (5 ml)

**Saturated fat per muffin – fat in egg may be disregarded
if eaten in small quantities**

**Unsaturated oil in entire quantity of lemon frosting –
1 tsp (5 ml)**

Saturated fat in lemon frosting – may be disregarded

NOTE: If you want to colour the icing, and your children cannot eat colourings, add a few drops of beetroot juice to the frosting to turn it bright pink.

squash, pineapple and oat muffins

Reminiscent of carrot muffins, these crunchy, moist, dairy-free muffins are my favourite!

MAKES 9 SMALL MUFFINS

½ cup (125 ml) rolled oats
½ cup (125 ml) wholemeal flour
½ tsp (2.5 ml) bicarbonate of soda
¾ tsp (4 ml) ground cinnamon
¼ tsp (1 ml) ground ginger
⅛ tsp ground nutmeg
⅛ tsp ground cloves
1 large egg, whisked
2 Tbsp (30 ml) cold-pressed sunflower oil
2 Tbsp (30 ml) honey
1 cup (250 ml) grated squash
⅓ cup (80 ml) grated pineapple
¼ cup (60 ml) raisins
4 Tbsp (60 ml) pecan nuts, chopped

Preheat the oven to 180 °C (350 °F). Oil a muffin tin. In a medium-sized bowl, mix together the oats, flour, bicarbonate of soda, cinnamon, ginger, nutmeg and cloves. Stir in the egg, oil and honey, then add the butternut, pineapple, raisins and pecans and mix. Spoon the mixture into the muffin tin and bake for about 20 minutes or until a skewer comes out clean. Turn out onto a wire rack to cool.

FAT AND OIL CONTENT OF ENTIRE BATCH
Unsaturated oil – 9 tsp (45 ml) – about 1 tsp (5 ml) per muffin
Saturated fat – 1 tsp (5 ml)

rich fruit cake

This moist, low-fat fruit cake can be jollied up at Christmas time with a generous soaking of brandy. The bright red cherries aren't exactly health food, but it's just not the same without them! Of course, if you don't like cherries, just leave them out.

MAKES 1 LOAF

250 g fruit cake mix and 250 g dates
(OR 500 g fruit cake mix)
1 scant cup (225 ml) pecan nuts
½ cup (125 ml) glacé cherries (optional)
1–2 Tbsp (15–30 ml) finely chopped fresh ginger
(optional)
1 generous mug (300 ml) rooibos tea
1 large egg, beaten
2 cups (500 ml) wholemeal flour
1 Tbsp (15 ml) baking powder (aluminium-free)

In a large mixing bowl, mix together the fruit, nuts, cherries (if using), fresh ginger (if using) and rooibos tea. Cover the bowl with a plate (not clingfilm) and leave the mixture to stand overnight, or at least for a couple of hours. When ready to bake, preheat the oven to 180 °C (350 °F).

Oil the loaf tin (non-aluminium) and shake a handful of flour around the inside to coat it well.

Mix the egg, flour and baking powder into the fruit-nut mixture and pour it into the loaf tin. Bake for 1 hour.

If the crust starts getting too well done, anchor a piece of aluminium foil under the tin and arrange it so that it comes up and over the crust (without touching it) to protect it from the heat. After 1 hour, reduce the heat to 150 °C (300 °F) and bake for another 15 minutes, or until a skewer comes out clean.

FAT AND OIL CONTENT OF ENTIRE LOAF
Unsaturated oil – 10 tsp (50 ml) – eat in moderation
Saturated fat – 1 tsp (5 ml)

moist carob and coffee cake

Carob is a powder made from the pods of an evergreen Mediterranean tree. It is a superb chocolate substitute, is healthy, naturally sweet, low in fat and packed with minerals. This cake is as close as you are going to get to a low-fat, healthy chocolate cake. Nevertheless, don't even think chocolate when you try this! The flavour definitely improves by the next day so try not to eat it in one sitting.

MAKES 9 SLICES

cake

1 tsp (5 ml) instant coffee granules
¼ cup (60 ml) boiling water
¼ cup (60 ml) carob powder
1½ cups (375 ml) wholemeal flour
1 Tbsp (15 ml) skimmed milk powder (optional)
½ tsp (2.5 ml) bicarbonate of soda
½ tsp (2.5 ml) cinnamon
½ tsp (2.5 ml) vanilla extract
¼ cup (60 ml) cold-pressed sunflower oil
1 large egg
¼ cup (60 ml) honey
¾ cup (190 ml) grated apple
3–4 Tbsp (45–60 ml) filtered water

sauce

¼ cup (125 ml) nuts (pecans, for example), very finely chopped in a food processor until 'powdered'
¼ cup (60 ml) skimmed milk powder OR
6 Tbsp (90 ml) more 'powdered' nuts
¼ cup (60 ml) carob powder
2 Tbsp (30 ml) honey
¾ cup (190 ml) water
¼ cup (60 ml) strong black coffee
½ tsp (2.5 ml) vanilla extract

Preheat the oven to 180 °C (350 °F).

To make the cake, dissolve the coffee granules in the boiling water and set aside to cool completely.

In a mixing bowl, combine the carob powder, flour, milk powder (if using), bicarbonate of soda and cinnamon. Add the vanilla extract, oil, egg and honey. Mix briefly. Stir in the apple, cooled coffee and water. The mixture must not be too runny – add the water slowly and check consistency all the time.

Pour the mixture into a medium-sized baking dish (about 20 x 20 cm) (don't use a tin), and bake for 25 minutes, or until a skewer comes out clean.

To make the sauce, combine the powdered nuts, milk powder (if using), carob powder, honey and a few tablespoons of the water in a pan. Mix well to form a smooth paste before adding the remaining water and the black coffee. Heat gently (do not boil), stirring constantly, until the sauce is well combined and smooth.

Allow the cake to cool a little and then prick it all over with a fork and cut it into slices. Pour the sauce over the cake and let it seep down between the slices.

FAT AND OIL CONTENT OF ENTIRE CAKE

Unsaturated oil – 18 tsp (90 ml) – eat in moderation
Unsaturated oil in extra nuts (if using) – 4 tsp (20 ml)
Saturated fat – 1 tsp (5 ml)

MY PANTRY

Here is a list of the products and brands I use in my recipes. herb salt is my favourite way of adding flavour to my dishes. Do try to get some to ensure the same results.

PRODUCT	AVAILABLE FROM
Baking powder (aluminium-free)	healthfood shops
Barley grass powder	healthfood shops
Beetroot juice capsules	healthfood shops
Butter beans, canned (no additives)	supermarkets
Carob powder	healthfood shops
Chickpeas	healthfood shops, supermarkets
Chutney	supermarkets
Cottage cheese, fat-free (no preservatives)	supermarkets, healthfood shops
Curry powder (mild, no irritants)	supermarkets
Flour, wholemeal	supermarkets
Flour, gluten-free high-fibre	healthfood shops, some supermarkets
Flour, gluten-free pancake and crumpet	healthfood shops
Fruit juice	supermarkets
Garam masala, unroasted	healthfood shops, supermarkets
Guar gum	healthfood shops
Herb salt	healthfood shops
Honey, raw	healthfood shops

PRODUCT	AVAILABLE FROM
Honey, raw	healthfood shops
Jam (no sugar added)	healthfood shops, supermarkets
Ketjap manis (aromatic soy sauce)	speciality food shops, some supermarkets
Milk powder, skimmed	supermarkets
Mustard powder (no additives)	healthfood shops
Oats, rolled	supermarkets
Oil, linseed (cold-pressed)	healthfood shops
Oil, olive (extra virgin cold-pressed)	supermarkets
Oil, sesame (cold-pressed)	healthfood shops
Oil, sunflower (cold-pressed)	healthfood shops, saupermarkets
Pasta, rye	supermarkets, healthfood shops
Peanut butter, non-hydrogenated	healthfood shops
Polenta	supermarkets
Sambal oelek (Indonesian chilli relish)	speciality food shops,some supermarkets
Sesame rye crispbread	supermarkets, healthfood shops
Seasoning, garlic and herb	supermarkets, healthfood shops
Seasoning, rosemary and sage	supermarkets, healthfood shops
Sorghum meal porridge, unrefined	healthfood shops
Soy sauce (MSG-free)	healthfood shops, most supermarkets
Tahini (sesame seed paste)	healthfood shops some supermarkets
Tomato passata (no additives)	supermarkets
Tomato purée (no additives)	supermarkets
Vanilla extract (nature identical)	healthfood shops, supermarkets
Wheat flakes (no sugar added)	supermarkets
Yoghurt, fat-free (no preservatives)	supermarkets

INDEX

Page numbers in *italics* indicate illustrations